Single
Parenting

SINGLE PARENTING

• • •

ROBERT G. BARNES, JR.

Living Books®
Tyndale House Publishers, Inc.
Wheaton, Illinois

ISBN 0-8423-5920-6
Library of Congress Card Catalog Number 92-64309

Printed in the United States of America

98 97 96 95
8   7   6   5

Acknowledgments

This book has become a reality thanks to many hands. The building blocks used to create this work were provided by numerous contributors who, through the years, have had a profound impact on my life. Initially, a very crucial time for me was while I was growing up in a single-parent home. My own widowed father never gave up on me, even when I gave up on myself. While I was no longer responding to his love, my single parent worked steadfastly at training me and thus sketched the first blueprints for the construction of this book.

More recently six people have played significant roles in the construction of this book; each has offered special input. My mother-in-law and father-in-law, the Reverend and Mrs.

90092

Glen Johnson, discipled me during my early Christian years. The opportunity I had to observe their personal sacrifices for what they believe in has been a lifetime inspiration to me. The Reverend Bill Billingsley, my pastor since 1974, has been used by God to add numerous spiritual building blocks to my life. As I sat before his pulpit, the bold truths of Scripture he revealed became a core for my philosophy of life.

The actual writing of the book came to fruition because of the help of men like Dr. Frank Shrader. As my major adviser in graduate school, he noticed my interest in the topic of single parenting and encouraged me to study it as a dissertation topic. Dr. O. S. Hawkins challenged and encouraged me to share the results of my research with people in seminar settings. From a distance of three hundred miles, the Reverend Ronald Palmer spent time encouraging me to put my seminar material into book form. These six friends have been used by God to help me put my thoughts into writing, and for this I am indebted.

A book, like a building, cannot become a reality without dedicated laborers. The staff at Sheridan House Ministries offered me invaluable professional input on this topic. Sheridan

House itself, which has provided residential care for approximately one thousand children from predominantly single-parent homes, offered me inexhaustible resources for study. Lillian Hughes, my secretary, has also been a great boon to me, working extra hours enthusiastically as if it were her own book.

There is generally one specific individual that God uses as a focal point of strength in a work such as this. In my case, it has been my wife, Rosemary. Throughout the year that it took me to write this book, she spent time clearing my schedule, reading and rereading my material, and constantly encouraging me toward its completion. As in all areas of my life, God has used her in a mighty way to help me in my service to him.

Contents

Foreword

The 1980 census revealed that there had been many shifts in American society during the decade of the seventies. One of the more profound sociological changes was shown to be the striking escalation in the number of single-parent homes.

At the time of the writing of this book, 90 percent of the single-parent families in America had single mothers, rather than single fathers, as the head of the family. The advice and counsel offered in this book can be used with equal effectiveness by single parents of either gender.

To make this book more readable, I have chosen to refer to the single mother because her gender predominates in single-parent families in general. In light of this, I do not want to be accused of ignoring the plight of the single father. I myself am the product of a home headed by a single father. The choice of gender was generally made to help the reader move more smoothly through the concepts of this book. My hat goes off, and my heart goes out, to all single parents, regardless of their sex.

Part One

◆ ◆ ◆

The First Wilderness Journey: Finding Your Self

1

Who
Am I?

Many situations in life confront us, screaming
for our assistance. We want to step out to help
but may find our own selves in need of help. Our
attempt at aiding another person is thus foiled.

"How can I help my children understand
why our family has fallen apart when I don't
really understand why it all happened as it
did?" This statement, which is so common for
the single parent to express, very likely captures the way Moses must have felt after being
forced out into the wilderness alone.

Here was a young man in the prime of his
life, having been raised in the palace of Pharaoh—perhaps one of the most prestigious

places in all the world at that time. On that particular day described in Exodus 2:11-12, Moses stepped out and decided to help his "children," the Israelites. He seemed to go about it without a plan or even much thought. All he knew was that "his children" were in desperate need of help.

Moses went about the task of helping the Israelites when he himself needed guidance in understanding his role. The people of Israel had no direction at this point, and Moses wanted to show them the way, when he himself was without direction. In his insecurity, Moses began his job of "parenting" almost as if he, too, were a child. "Moses looked this way and that to be sure no one was watching" (Exodus 2:12). Here we have a clear portrayal of an adolescent wanting to do something, but unsure of how to go about it, so he looks all around to make sure he is not seen. Moses was in the prime of his life when he stepped out that day. Why did he perform a task like an insecure teenager and then, as the story continues, run away from home? Can an adult go through adolescence again?

The stage of life we label "adolescence" has many facets to it. First of all, it is a *physical* process ushered in by puberty. The body goes through many biological changes to bring a person from childhood to adulthood. Second, adolescence is a *social* process. The child is no longer in such a limited world as he goes to school and moves from class to class developing many more relationships than he had in the self-contained classroom of the elementary school. The teenager's life is not as structured as it was in the past, and he is forced to make many more decisions.

Dealing with such decisions is a new responsibility, and he often feels inept because of a lack of experience in the decision-making process. This ineptitude helps to bring about the third aspect of adolescence, the *emotional* state. As the teenager is faced with all these new changes, situations, decisions, and responsibilities, he goes through the emotional upheaval brought on by insecurity, doubt, and self-examination.

"I thought I knew who I was. My role in life was so set, but now it seems like I'm searching to find me."

This statement sounds as if it had been made by a teenager, but it was actually made by an adult. Though we do not repeat the physical aspects of adolescence, many times in our lives circumstances temporarily force us back into the emotional feelings of an adolescent.

There was a time in my life when I was job-hunting. One interview after another and one rejection after another began to have a major effect on the way I felt about myself. The interviews were new situations for me, and the rejections made me feel less and less secure. Often it was obvious that the rejections had nothing to do with me. It was either the wrong kind of job for me, or there were simply no openings; but still I treated them as personal rejections. I had begun the interview process without a plan and without even deciding what I expected as an outcome. In my insecurity, I was walking through the situation with the emotions of an adolescent.

This is much the same way that the "single again" person begins his new life. He is forced into the role of single parent before he has dealt with the realities of being single. These are separate adjustments: "single again" being an emotional state to overcome, and "single parenting" being a role or function. One cannot effectively fulfill the role of a nurturing parent until one has dealt with the primary and personal state of being single.

A wilderness land can be a beautiful retreat into solitude and nature for those experienced travelers who journey there just for that reason. For others who end up in the wilderness through no choice of their own, it is a lonely, barren place with cactus, snakes, lizards, and vultures. For these travelers the wilderness climate is not a beautiful picture of the Creator's contrasts, but rather a frighteningly dramatic climate of sweltering days and bitterly cold nights.

Many caravan through this desolate terrain. Some are able to find a path, stick to it, and eventually arrive at the end of the wilderness. For others, however, the wilderness journey is more treacherous. These travelers become wilderness nomads, because they are unable to remain in a consistent direction.

By far, the most recurring feeling expressed by the "single again" is the loneliness. "As long as I stay busy, doing anything, I'm OK. But when I sit in my bedroom at the end of the day and stare at the walls, I get a knot in my stomach I'm so lonely." This was the way one woman expressed her feelings. Once again, like a teenager, the single individual feels that she is groping to find her place in the world around her. Even though people such as friends and family may express their love, a barren feeling still exists inside. The emptiness is so vast it seems to be endless. "How many nights will I wind up in this room crying?"

In this emotional state of mind every challenge in life seems like an attack by a serpent, and the "single again" often feels that she is simply bouncing from the bristles of one cactus to the next. The everyday difficulties—car problems, illness, or disciplining the children—become major hurdles. Just as it is difficult for a traveler to share large amounts of water when he is in a desert, it is also difficult for one who is emotionally drained and thirsty to give continually to those around him. Soon small problems needing attention begin to look like attacking vipers instead.

The constant fluctuation in the climate is but another difficulty to be dealt with in the wilderness. If the single person could only count on and prepare for just one type of circumstance—a moderate temperature—the task would be easier. However, the extremes of day and night, coupled with the storms, are too much to bear. "Just as I've had the happiest day that I've had in months, the roof seems to cave in." It is difficult to learn to weather the emotions caused by the extremes in life's events. Often the single person feels unable to handle another storm.

The hardest part about the wilderness journey, however, is finding a way out of this barren existence. When will the morning bring a horizon with lush vegetation or any comfort and relief? Not just an oasis that will not be there tomorrow and not a mirage, but a genuinely lasting change in one's life out of the scorching existence? In what direction can it be found or which path should be followed?

The next three chapters will focus on these three aspects of the wilderness: loneliness, emotional climate, and direction. Moses first had to conquer the wilderness himself before he could walk his people through this troubled journey.

2

I'm
All Alone

In her book *Parent Alone,* Suzanne Stewart talks about the shock of being left by her husband. She had three children to raise, but that was not the biggest load she had to carry. "Fear and panic dominated my feelings," she writes. "I wanted to cry to the world, 'Help!' but the world didn't care." The biggest problem she faced was the reality of being alone, not just the added burden of the responsibilities that used to be handled by two people and now had to be shouldered by one.

"No! John can't leave me forever. He loves me, and the children. I know he does!" These were the thoughts she kept coming back to as a way of dealing with her aloneness.

The shock of the first step into this wilderness is often one of disbelief. "I can't believe this is happening to me. I keep thinking that maybe I'll wake up and find out that this is just a bad dream." These are often the initial thoughts of newly divorced mothers and fathers.

Ann is a young woman who grew up in a typical middle-class home, did well in high school, and after one year of college married her high-school sweetheart. She never had the opportunity to grow out of adolescence emotionally and become an independent, mature adult, because she married at nineteen and transferred her dependence from her father to her new husband. There was never a time in Ann's life when she was alone and responsible for major decisions beyond day-to-day situations.

At nineteen, Ann had fairy-tale illusions of marriage. Television and romantic novels had made it seem as if no work or effort were involved because "love conquers all." Once you got married everything would be wonderful. Four years and two babies later, Ann found herself walking the path that Moses had walked the day he ran from Egypt. For four months she was in shock, refusing to believe that she had been left alone. Finally, Ann began to accept the reality that her husband was not coming back.

By accepting the reality of her singleness, Ann had taken the first step, but not without anguish. For a while, she decided to remain in the wilderness. Being alone with all its pain was better than going out and risking any new friendships.

As an emotional "adolescent," the young mother had become very self-conscious. She related, "I felt as if everyone was staring at me." Ann was reacting like a young teenager walking down the school halls with her first big pimple. She was convinced that everyone could see the pimple and that its existence was the talk of the school. In reality everyone else was too busy coping with his own blemishes and personal traumas to know her problem even existed. By returning to emotional adolescence, Ann became her own worst enemy. Not wanting to face other people and feeling unlovable, she actually increased her loneliness.

Imagine the change that instantly took place in Moses' life—from a life of festivities, crowds, wealth, and prestige to nothingness. Having been raised by the Pharaoh's daughter may have meant he was a man of power. Certainly he was never alone. Now he had made a decision to run away and in doing so was alone in the wilderness.

As the account continues, Moses was in the wilderness, sitting down against the well and pouting. Later he helped the girls at the well. They told their father, Reuel, who invited Moses to dinner. *The Living Bible* says, "Moses eventually decided to accept Reuel's invitation" (Exodus 2:21). His thoughts might have been like Ann's. He had had enough of relationships or even friendships for a while, and he wanted to be alone and pity himself in the wilderness.

So often, the "single again," while trying to accept loneliness, makes decisions that cause her to be even more alone. In her teenagelike self-consciousness, she is afraid to leave her little spot in the wilderness. The thought of having to deal with people is as frightening as meeting some of those reptiles in the wilderness. Little insignificant comments from well-meaning friends are often misinterpreted and cut her like a sharp cactus. So lonely she could die of thirst, she is afraid to risk tasting the water.

Scripture records that Moses *eventually* decided to accept Reuel's invitation. Ann, also, *eventually* decided to deal with her loneliness by venturing out. Still feeling that no one could know what she was going through, Ann had to find someone with whom she could talk. Unfortunately, Ann's first decision was to once again look for someone to become dependent on, rather than a person with whom she could share.

Long before Ann walked or even crawled around in the wilderness she was in, she got up and started running. Trying to forget her loneliness, Ann began dating. After her first date she found herself responding like a teenager. High expectations and the fantasy of someone to lean on caused her to rush into an involvement she was not at all prepared to handle. Ann had not yet learned to be alone or to accept that single state of being. She was simply trying to avoid growing out of adolescence.

Dating a man who was also divorced, Ann eventually realized they had nothing in common. She was just avoiding the problem, trying to live in the fairy tale in which Mr. Right would come riding over the horizon on a beautiful white horse, scoop her up (with an arm big enough to scoop the two children, too), and ride off to his castle. She would then never be troubled again. Of course she would once again be dependent on another person. Ann wanted someone to trust, someone who could empathize with her pain and lead her out of the wilderness—today. In this state of mind, she was bound to make bad decisions. She was turning to a person rather than to the Creator of persons.

Eventually Ann realized that the man she was dating had been lost in the wilderness even longer than she. An in-depth romantic relationship would just whitewash her loneliness and pain. Something else had to happen. In her search Ann was desperate and now willing to run risks. She sat down one night and examined the available options. She knew she could meet people at bars or in a bowling league, but those people seemed as if they would once again just cause her to avoid dealing with her loneliness. There were organizations such as Parents without Partners, but her one encounter with their meetings had left her more concerned with finding partners than with being parents. Ann had been on that road and it led nowhere. The third option was to visit a church she had heard about in her town.

A friend told Ann that a downtown church was concerned about people who were divorced and had formed a "Single Again" Sunday school department. Ann had never been involved with a church before except at Christmas and Easter. The thought of facing the future alone, however, was frightening enough to cause her to risk a different experience.

Ann's expectations of what this church experience would be like heightened her "adolescent" anxieties. Early that Sunday morning as she was preparing herself and her children to go to the church, Ann kept asking herself, *Why am I doing this? These people will probably all just stare at me as if I had some communicable disease.* The adolescent in her was coming out again. Her self-consciousness made her believe that all the people she would meet at the Singles Department would be smiling, have life all put together with no problems and no blemishes. These thoughts almost caused her to stay home.

Similarly Moses might have thought it was a mistake to go to the house of Reuel. After all, this man was a shepherd, and Moses was a city dweller from Pharaoh's house. How could they identify with each other?

Now, Ann's desperate loneliness kept her moving toward church. Walking in the door that the usher pointed to was one of the most difficult moves Ann had ever taken. *All they have to do is look at me, and they'll be able to tell all the things I've been through,* she thought. At the end of that hour Ann learned that part of her prediction was true. It was an hour of Bible study, sharing, and both laughing and crying. As Ann listened to others share, she realized for the first time in months that she was not alone.

Without saying a word, Ann was forced to tears because she could identify so closely with the testimonies she was hearing. People were willing to share about their own lonely journey through the wilderness, without the façade. Ann was correct in thinking that the people would all know what she was going through. They could empathize with her pain, because many had also been there or were in a similar experience at that time.

Ann left the church that day with new hope. She was not quite sure what the hope was based on; after all, the people she had met had been members there for some time. Even though they seemed to have a special joy, they were also still feeling pain. She could hardly wait for next Sunday.

Over the next several weeks Ann was able to learn many lessons about being alone. The most important difference she saw in these new friends was their dependence. They were not depending on another person or on a relationship to get them out of the wilderness. It was their dependence on God that seemed to be pulling them through the wilderness. They were allowing God to meet their needs through faith in his unconditional love.

Two thousand years ago the disciples of Jesus Christ were also forced into realizing their need to depend totally on him. They were sailing on the boat while Christ was sleeping in the bow. A storm came up, and since most of them were fishermen, they tried to deal with the storm themselves. As the storm became more violent, their faith in their own abilities waned. They hoped that the boat would weather the storm. It did not take them long to realize theirs was a misplaced faith. Only as a last resort did the disciples call on the Lord to save them. Dependence on their own abilities or on the quality of their boat was not enough to save them.

Truths from this story can easily apply to loneliness. First, one may have confidence in his or her own ability to handle a crisis. As that fails, the next step is often dependence on outside situations like a job, a new relationship, and so on. When the shallowness of that kind of faith is seen for what it is, then many turn to a faith in Jesus Christ. In his love for us, he often will not intervene until called upon. Our Lord understands the wilderness, since he himself knew the rigors and its temptations while he was on this earth. For us to attempt to handle the journey without him, however, is to put our faith in something other than Christ.

Ann began to learn that lesson. She found that the wilderness could not be conquered overnight. It was a matter of putting one foot in front of the other and walking in one direction only—toward Christ. In order to do this, Ann began meeting once a week with a prayer partner, another single mother. As they shared together, Ann was also able to talk to someone she could trust about many of the details and worries of being single. They could discuss the usual problems of money, security, business matters, and more importantly, the children. Having someone once again to discuss and pray about these things with was a big relief. Most of all that person would not create a dependent relationship, but point that dependence toward God.

While the sharing and growing continued, Ann realized that her spiritual development was somehow being hindered. She had other things with which to deal. She was now ready to look at the changing climate in her wilderness, especially the bitterness and the guilt.

IN REVIEW
Principles for Overcoming Loneliness
1. Accept the reality of being alone without any dreams or illusions.
2. Don't look for someone or something to become dependent upon.
3. Transfer your faith and dependence to God.
4. Find a prayer partner—someone you trust—to share with.
5. Don't expect an answer to the loneliness to come tomorrow.
6. Trust in God and wait on his love.

3

Why Me?

The "single again" journey, among other things, is a grief process. During this time of sorrow and loss the single parent must go through several emotional stages. After surveying nearly six hundred single parents at a single-parent workshop that I conducted in 1981, I was struck by the specific nature of these emotional stages. One question I asked was "How long have you been divorced or separated?" A second question was phrased to help us ascertain what emotional feeling or pain the single parent was experiencing in her attempt to cope. Four very definite stages appeared to coincide with the length of time that one was separated from a spouse.

As discussed in chapter 2, the first emotion to cope with is loneliness. The second stage is bitterness, and the third stage involves guilt. The fourth stage of emotion following divorce is one of acknowledging a need to do something about the situation, to plan for the future. (This planning stage will be the subject of chapter 4.)

The wilderness has bitterly cold nights that are so sharp they cut through clothing. The bitterness that can develop by being left alone with the children can also cut through a person's heart. However, that emotion persists, cutting everything in sight, including other people. Once one has accepted being single again—often in an effort to cope—the person begins to seek a scapegoat, someone she can lash out against in an effort to place the blame somewhere.

The most logical person to attack first is the ex-spouse. "It wasn't like me to act like I did during the divorce. I just found myself wanting him to hurt the way I was hurting." This was the confession Martha made when she came to the counseling center for help. The coldness goes so deep and so intense that the bitter person begins to exert incredible energy against her target.

In his book *How to Help a Friend,* Paul Welter describes the bitter person as first focusing her venom on one target, such as an ex-spouse. Soon the venom seems to spread out to everyone around her. "The bitter person is abrasive to anyone who happens by, but most abrasive to people who are close. As a friend of mine says, 'He [the bitter person] is the kind of person who would stroke a cat from the tail to the head'" (p. 102).

Once again, as during the loneliness stage, the bitterness stage is self-perpetuating. As people reached out to help and befriend Martha, it didn't take long for her to transfer her venom toward the new friends. The bitter person soon alienates herself.

Martha wanted to know how she could help her children overcome the bitterness they felt toward their father because he never visited. "He doesn't even call them at Christmas. Now, how can we help not being bitter about that?" The key was not the children, but rather, the "we" in her statement. Martha first had to deal with the bitterness she had toward her ex-husband before she could help the children. The husband was not the key issue in Martha's reaction either. Long after the thorn has been removed from the hand, the hand itself must be cared for. Martha's focus needed to be on the infection in her own heart. She needed to examine her own reactions, her own hurts, and her own bitterness.

In the bitterness stage it did not take long for Martha's bitterness toward her ex-husband to develop into a bitterness toward life in general and finally toward God himself.

"Why have you done this to me, God?"

"And they turned against Moses, whining, 'Have you brought us out here to die in the desert? . . . Why did you make us leave Egypt?'" *(Exodus 14:11)*.

The children of Israel were scared and bitter. They were focusing their bitterness toward Moses, but it was really aimed at God. God was the one who had brought them to that point in their journey. They were so bitter toward God that they could no longer envision the land of milk and honey; they could focus only on the problems of the moment.

Quite often people think that their own personal bitterness toward God is justified. Unfortunately, they spend most of their lives in this stage of the journey. Some may remain bitter to the very end. Others, such as Martha, are aware of their bitterness, but not aware that they are expressing this attitude toward God. Our Lord cannot communicate with us when we harbor this sin.

Acknowledgment that this bitterness exists, confession of it, and then a dedication to getting closer to God and his love are the necessary steps to healing. God's love is an antithesis of bitterness and also its antidote. The two opposing forces of love and bitterness could not coexist within Martha. With an act of her will she had to choose between the two forces; God would not do this for her.

In order to evict her bitter feelings and be controlled by God's love, Martha needed to spend time in prayer and study. For Martha to truly overcome her bitter feelings and keep them from returning, she had to return to the point at which the bitterness had begun. Martha had to forgive her ex-husband, not because he asked for forgiveness (which he did not), but because it was a step with God that she had to take. This is a long and difficult step. Martha had to commit her ex-husband to prayer and with God's help, conquer the angry feelings she had toward him. (If Martha did not allow her closeness to God to help her remove *all* bitterness, eventually these feelings would return. In a short period of time, the temporarily suppressed bitterness would emerge. It is similar to the cancer surgeon who wants to be sure he has removed all of the malignancy so that it will not grow back stronger.)

Is this bitterness conquered overnight or next week? No! After all, this bitterness stage does not take twenty-four hours to develop. It takes time to overcome, and it must be replaced by a stronger relationship with Christ. For the children of Israel the journey in the wilderness took time—forty years, to be exact. Though agonizing, that time span was not as significant as the final outcome—a new land and a new way of life. The journey through bitter weather and near the bitter springs will take time. It takes time to love again and to find God's path. The key is not to waste time, but to spend it with God.

IN REVIEW
Principles for Overcoming Bitterness
1. Remember that bitterness toward other people eventually results in bitterness toward God.

2. Bitterness blocks access to God.
3. Allow God's love to overcome bitterness.
4. Just as you are forgiven, you must forgive those around you.
5. It takes time, God's quality time, to be free from bitterness.

4

I Deserve It

At a certain point in the wilderness journey
the traveler looks at all that has transpired
and decides, *I probably deserve what I'm going
through.* This is the feeling that one has done
many things wrong and therefore deserves to
be punished. Guilt is an amazingly strong
force. Dr. Hyder, in his book *The Christian's
Handbook of Psychiatry,* says it is a "mixture
of emotions and thoughts which destroy inner
peace" (p. 113).

"I've gotten to the point where I can't even
face myself anymore. I've ruined so many lives,
and so many good things have gone bad because
of me. How could even God forgive me?" These

were the pleadings of a young single parent in my office. The feelings of guilt are, unfortunately, a very common form of emotional and spiritual cancer.

Dr. Hyder writes that guilt often becomes so overbearing that many people become physically ill as a form of self-punishment. If the physical pain is removed by medical treatment, but not the guilt, then another physical malady will develop shortly to take the place of the original illness. Guilt can be the root of many crippling illnesses. To successfully treat such illnesses, one must work at the root level.

In today's world, many secular psychologists believe that guilt itself should be eradicated. They say that a person should strive to feel no guilt, regardless of his actions. To acknowledge that there is any value to guilt over one's behavior would be to admit that there is an ultimate right or wrong. The secular therapist believes that guilt of any kind is unhealthy and that the principle of right and wrong changes from person to person. The Christian, on the other hand, must accept guilt as a reality and must ask for forgiveness for the action that caused it. Only then can Christ's power overcome the guilt.

There are two sets of rules in this world:

man's rules and God's rules. When one breaks
man's rules, he is prosecuted and either con-
victed or acquitted. When a man breaks God's
rules, he is punished eternally. There is
another alternative however; the man can
humble himself, ask for forgiveness, and then
be sent out of God's "courtroom" innocent. A
penalty had to be paid for the violation, but
Christ died on the cross to pay the price for
each of us. Guilt must be dealt with. The
choice is to fight it or to understand that it is
part of the reason Jesus Christ died.

There are daily words, thoughts, and deeds
in our lives over which we could continually
feel guilty. However, we can repent of our
transgressions and move on with our lives,
knowing we are forgiven (Psalm 103:10-12).
To deny the availability of this forgiveness is to
deny the very death and resurrection of Jesus
Christ. He was not just a man who lived a
great life and died a cruel death. Christ was the
perfect God-Man who came down from his
throne because of our guilt. With our sin we
became guilty. When we accept his death on
that cross as payment in full for all our sin,
God judges us as innocent: "He personally carried the load of our sins in his own body when
he died on the cross, so that we can be finished

with sin and live a good life from now on. For his wounds have healed ours" (1 Peter 2:24).

The single parent will remain in the guilt stage until as a Christian she realizes that the ongoing feeling of guilt (after it has been given to Christ) is itself a sin. The woman I mentioned who came to my office might have felt guilty about something in her past: her marriage, the divorce, or the trauma experienced by her children. It was time, however, to give all of the guilt to Christ and move ahead in her spiritual walk, affirming her forgiveness. Maybe she did not feel confident that Christ could forgive her for the sins that she had committed. Possibly, this woman felt that she was such an incredible sinner that she had to remain guilty and punish herself.

Moses the murderer was forgiven and eventually followed God out of the wilderness. David the adulterer and murderer was also forgiven. Peter who denied he even knew Christ overcame his guilt when he realized that he had been forgiven. A Samaritan woman went to the well to get water at an unusual time of day probably to avoid people (John 4:7-26), since she carried the guilt of having been married five times, and was at that point living with another man out of wedlock. She also found freedom from her guilt when Christ forgave her. No longer fearing to meet people from her town because of her guilt, she marched in to announce her newfound joy.

These examples of triumph over feelings of guilt are not the prime reason to know that Christ is the forgiver of all our sins. First John 1:9 gives us the formula: "But if we confess our sins to him, he can be depended on to forgive us and to cleanse us from every wrong. [And it is perfectly proper for God to do this for us because Christ died to wash away our sins.]" To continue to punish yourself and to continue feeling guilty after you have asked for forgiveness is to say that this verse (and thus the Bible) is a lie or that God just is not capable of forgiving what you have done. Christ came to earth precisely because you and I are sinners.

The guilt you feel is to help you humble yourself and acknowledge your need for forgiveness. There is no punishment you may inflict upon yourself to atone for your sins. To attempt to do so is to insult Christ and what he went through on the cross. Instead, confess and then accept the forgiveness paid for by Christ. Do not hold on to the guilt after the sin has been paid for by Christ's sacrifice. As it is said in 1 Peter 2:24: let Christ carry the load of our sin and guilt. That is why he came. Now get on with your life. He has something good in store for you!

IN REVIEW
Principles for Understanding Guilt
1. Everyone experiences guilt because of the words, thoughts, or deeds of daily life.
2. Guilt is a spiritual difficulty.
3. Sin must be paid for.
4. Christ gave his life to pay the price for sin.
5. To be forgiven of sin, you must personally accept the payment that Christ's death offers.
6. Once you have asked for and accepted forgiveness, there is no further reason to feel guilty. Your sins have been forgiven.
7. Rest in the comfort of Matthew 11:28: "Come unto me, all ye that labour and are heavy laden, and I will give you rest" (KJV).

5

Out of the Wilderness

"I've been in this rut and confusion for so long that I've almost become used to it," Linda confessed one day in my office. "There is no direction in my life or my home. I just run from one crisis to the next." Studies indicate that Linda is part of a dramatically expanding portion of the population in America today.

The 1980 census reported that nine out of every ten single-parent homes are headed by a mother rather than a father and that the number of these homes in America is phenomenal! The same census also showed that 42 percent of the households in America are headed by a woman (many of these are older widows along with single mothers). The magnitude of the situation is staggering.

When Linda came to see me, she wasn't concerned with statistics, however. She was saying that she was tired of wandering around in the wilderness with no direction. She knew that it was time to begin the journey out—this time with God's help.

Moses had tried to make it on his own, and was falling far short of his potential. He was not accomplishing anything close to what he could have for God. After his "burning bush" confrontation (Exodus 3) and his recommitment to God, he was ready to end his personal wandering and begin helping his "family." None of this happened overnight. Moses was unsure of himself and very unsure of the new positive step he was taking. He cried out to God several times, saying, "I can't do it!" God agreed with him. Moses could not have done it alone, but this time he followed the leadership of the Lord. Moses was able to begin walking out of the wilderness. When doubt surrounded him, he leaned on the special rod that God had prepared for him.

For the single parent the walk out of the wilderness is just as difficult. Linda had to take that first step to put her life back in order. She had begun to accept the fact that she was alone. With God's help she was overcoming her bitterness and guilt. It was time to turn to God for the future. Not only is God available to help us over the tragedies of our past, but also he wants to give us a new direction for the future. Linda needed the faith to know that she could lean on the "spiritual rod" of God as she began to walk out of her emotional wilderness.

God had given Moses a plan, and that is what Linda needed as well. She had never taken the time to look at her life or to examine her direction or to set her priorities. Linda had never put God at the center of her decisions. The first step that she needed to take was prayerfully to establish God's priorities for her. Then she could look at the hindrances in her path.

Linda's basic responsibilities in life boiled down to two roles that often conflicted. Was she to be a parent first or a provider first? Government studies show that the annual median income for a family headed by a married couple is $23,141 (*Newsweek*, January 17, 1983). The same study reported that the average female-headed household earns $9,320 annually. Dr. Christopher Jenks refers to today's single mother as "the new underclass" in our

social strata (*Family Weekly,* April 24, 1983).
Many of these women are unequipped and inexperienced when they enter today's job market.
To add to their difficulties, Dr. Jenks reports their earning power is only 57 percent that of their male counterparts.

"For a while Jack sent us child support, but eventually both he and the checks vanished," Linda sighed. Linda had become responsible for the feeding and support of her family, and yet it appeared that she was somewhat handicapped before she had even begun. This is a very typical dilemma. Studies show that paternal child-support payments, as well as visitation, decrease as time goes on. Only 35 percent of the mothers who are eligible for child support are getting anything at all, according to "When Divorce Divides a Family" (*Redbook,* April 1983, p. 67).

"I know I am supposed to spend more time with the children, but I also have to pay for the food. How do I do both?" Unfortunately, Linda had been in this indecisive limbo for three years. She had basically made a decision to make no decision at all. She took the first job that came along—working in a department store. Her income was not nearly enough to maintain the life-style her family had become accustomed to, but still she tried to continue doing everything, only to watch as things began falling apart. She even considered getting a second job. To start walking out of the wilderness, Linda needed guidance and a plan.

The plan for Linda became one of setting goals. That meant she had to learn to make decisions. In order to make sound decisions, one must learn how to analyze the specific situation. This means taking time out to sit down with pencil and paper, listing the pros and cons of the direction one wants to go in. Once this is done, it is always wise to seek the counsel of another adult. Quite often we do not realize the availability of experts who can be of immense help to us. In analyzing her financial condition, Linda recognized that it was not a matter of working or staying home. She had to work. Linda's concern was how to make her role of parent her number-one priority. How could she avoid having to work an additional job at night in order to pay the bills?

Financial advisers are available from many quarters. Most banks offer free counseling and literature to those who want help with personal finances. There are also books available. Linda, however, was guided toward another option. She went to her pastor, who in turn

approached an accountant in the church on
Linda's behalf. The accountant, along with his
wife, visited Linda and took a long hard look
at her financial situation and monthly budget.
It quickly surfaced that Linda had no monthly
budget, no guidelines, and no financial goals.
The Christian accountant also helped Linda
see that she could not possibly hope to maintain the same standard of living she had
before. To attempt to do so would become only
more and more frustrating. She needed to be
more realistic about what she could and could
not do financially. Over a series of several meetings, Linda was helped to make some financial
decisions and set realistic goals. Linda didn't
need a second job; she needed a plan and now
she had one.

One of the outgrowths of Linda's financial
planning had a profound impact on her family
and thus is worth mentioning. She was shown
a living arrangement that many other single
parents are getting involved in today. Through
her church Linda met several other women
who were heading their household. One of
these women became her prayer partner and
helped act as a sounding board as Linda began
making new decisions. After several months of
this relationship, Linda and the other mother

decided that it would benefit both families financially to move in with each other.

Was the adjustment that these two families had to make as they blended an easy one? No. A more significant question is "Did Linda have to get a second job?" No, she could now better afford to stay home in the evenings and be with her children. The income of the two working moms made that possible, and the divided household duties gave her more time.

The accountant helped Linda adopt a regular monthly budget to avoid her habit of impulse buying. She was forced to make some very difficult monetary decisions such as whether she could really afford private education for her children. All this guidance would have been wasted, however, if Linda had not made the decision to follow it. She needed a plan, and then she needed to follow it.

Linda's financial plan was built on the premise that money was not God's priority. "I had to decide that God wanted me to be with my children, not just buy things for them," Linda finally realized.

Establishing God's priority was really the key issue. Since God wants the single parent to be a parent before being a provider, then God can be counted on to make that possible. However, God does want us to use the mind and the abilities he has given us to accomplish this task, and that is what Linda began to do. Rather than going haphazardly from one crisis to the next, she began planning for her life.

The problem of finances is not the only obstacle that blocks the way out of the wilderness. Many other decisions and goals have to be analyzed. Dr. Charles Smith, in his book *Helps for the Single-Parent Christian Family* (Convention Press, Nashville, Tennessee, 1978), says that the single parent must examine her needs regularly. "Depriving yourself of having your needs met will keep your child from having a happy, well-adjusted parent," he warns, and then lists four areas in which goals need to be set rather than ignored:

1. *Physical Goals.* Often one of the first areas of life that a newly divorced parent allows to become undisciplined is the physical condition. Yet this is extremely important for both clear thinking and self-esteem. A diet and exercise program may be necessary. A realistic physical goal may include a specific weight or a time for jogging a mile. The key, however, is to be specific about the goal and plan for its success.

2. *Mental Goals.* Doing something to improve the mind is a worthy goal. Learning something new, reading a certain number of books this year, developing a new skill, such as typing or sales—all are worthy goals that will help to expand the horizon and increase opportunities for the single parent. Not only will these goals make her more interesting to be with, but they will also be an encouragement to the children.

3. *Social Goals.* This area means more than dating. In almost every geographical area there are dozens of places to go. On the weekend, newspapers list forthcoming community events. The goal should be to get out and do something socially. The plan could be to hunt for these social events and activities. The "single again" person needs to get in touch with her world before she can get in touch with the new people who come into her world.

4. *Spiritual Goals.* This is actually the most important area. A church with a nurturing study of God's Word should be found. Also it is mandatory for the single parent to establish her own personal daily Bible study. The goal is to get closer to God and find his will. The means to that end are daily prayer and Bible study.

Much more could be said about setting goals, but the key is not so much the goals. The important process is not even the plan and making the decision to do something to achieve these goals. Linda, as with many other single parents, had made countless promises to herself, setting her sights on many goals. This time, however, she was stepping out with God's spiritual staff at her side. Just as God gave Moses a staff, the spiritual staff will help Linda change the direction of her life.

A friend of mine is fond of a story about three frogs who were sitting on a log. Two frogs decided to jump off. How many were left? The response he always gets is that one frog is left, but that answer is incorrect. There were still three frogs on the log. The two frogs only "decided" to jump. They had not actually gone through with their decision. To Linda it was obviously time to jump rather than to sit on the same log she had been on for years.

Taking steps to leave the wilderness requires an understanding that God can show us the plan and help with the obstacles. Then it takes a commitment to put one foot in front of the other, day by day, to follow his plan. Linda started walking.

IN REVIEW
Principles for Walking out of the Wilderness
1. Pray about God's priorities for your life.
2. Accept the responsibilities and priorities God has put before you.
3. Establish goals.
4. Commit yourself to these goals.
5. Knowing that God will help you to fulfill his priorities for your life, take the first step and keep walking.

Part Two of this book is a discussion of goals for children and a plan to help the single parent obtain these goals.

Part Two

◆ ◆ ◆

The Second
Wilderness
Journey:
Leading
Your
Children

6

Train up a Child

Moses had not put his life completely back together, but he still returned to Egypt because he had heard the command of God (Exodus 3). In that "burning bush" experience, Moses had come to see that God wanted him to go back and lead the Israelites through the wilderness. As their leader, Moses did not have all the answers, but this time he did have a plan given to him by God. Now there was something different about this man. Moses had tried once before to help the people of Israel, but one of the Israelites had responded with a rejection: " 'And who are you?' the man demanded. 'I suppose you think you are *our* prince and judge! And do you plan to kill me as you did that Egyptian yesterday?'" (Exodus 2:14). Moses reacted by running away.

Moses may have thought he was doing the right thing or that he was helping; but when the Israelite criticized him, he responded to the criticism rather than out of his convictions. He allowed the opinion of others to sway him from his task. However, when Moses returned from his own personal wilderness journey, a new man could be seen. Once again Moses came to help the Israelites, and once again he was rejected and ridiculed: "When they [the Israelites] met Moses and Aaron waiting for them outside the palace, as they came out from their meeting with Pharaoh, they swore at them" (Exodus 5:20-21).

Moses had asked Pharaoh to let God's people go. Pharaoh had responded by forcing the Israelites to make bricks without the convenience of having the necessary straw. The Israelites, furious at Moses for instigating this, cursed him. Moses, however, did not abandon the task this time, but responded to something other than the complaints of those he was trying to help. He responded to what he knew to be God's will. He knew God wanted him to shepherd these people. The end result would be to their benefit. Three principles can be discerned here concerning Moses and his new way of responding:

1. Moses was aware that God had a task for him to do, and whether he liked it or not, he had to accept it.

2. Moses was now responding to the commands of God, rather than to the complaints of the Israelites.

3. Moses was focusing on God's promise of the end result for his people—the promised land—rather than the day-to-day difficulties.

God has a similar command for parents in general and single parents in particular. Much can be learned by following the example of Moses.

That brings us to Proverbs 22:6, which can be divided into three parts. The first part says, "Train up a child in the way he should go" (KJV). The single parent has so many other tasks that must be done in life that she often revises the beginning of this verse to read:

"If you would like to train up your child . . ."

or

"When you get time, train up your child . . ."

or

"If you know how, train up your child . . ."

or

"Provide your child with the things that he wants."

Here God is speaking in a very emphatic way. A parent *must* train up the child God has given her. This is a command. The fact that God commands a parent to train up a child is reason enough for the priority this task must take in life. There is no option and there are no special circumstances. God did not put a footnote in that verse to read, "unless, of course, you are a single parent." People who have children are commanded by God to train them.

In today's world of instant answers and instant foods, we have become accustomed to searching for simple solutions. Moses took the task despite its enormity, because he knew it was what God wanted him to do. He also knew that if God wanted him to do the job, God would supply him with the means and the abilities to get it done. Similarly, there is no easy way to train a child, especially a child trying to deal with the loss of a parent. There is no quick way to do it either. Too often, until a single parent becomes convinced that she is commanded to make parenting a priority, she will back away from this responsibility. The first step, then, is for each parent to commit herself to the task of training her child.

The word *train* as a noun can give us a helpful insight into this first priority. A train consists of a locomotive, which pulls many cars down a track. The train travels in one direction so that it is easy to see where the train is coming from and where it is heading. If one of the cars stops following the direction of the locomotive, there will be an accident. The planned destination will be reached only if all the cars are following the locomotive.

The same is true if we use the word *train* as a verb. When training a child, the "locomotive"—being the parent—must plan for and structure a series of learning experiences that are consistently heading down a track in one direction. Quite often the single parent attempts to train the child with one event or lecture. Many times there is no plan or direction, only a hasty attempt at crisis management: When a problem arises, the parent deals with it. With this sort of "training," the parenting is very random, inconsistent, and directionless. Training must be a series of ongoing, connecting events. If the track is too hard to follow, the lessons will be ineffective.

To train up a child, the parent must establish a plan. The remaining chapters of this book will help the single parent establish a plan (chapter 7) and will discuss the lessons that should be included in the training plan (chapters 8–20). Once a parent has adopted a plan, the real work begins. Each parent must start the uphill job of training, while staying on the track and going in one direction.

The second part of Proverbs 22:6 gives the parent a hint of what to expect during the training period: "and when he is old." It is both interesting and encouraging for the parent that the verse does not read, ". . . and when he is a child" or "when he is an adolescent, he will not depart from it." "When he is old" means that when the child is mature or an adult, he will not depart from the teachings of his parents.

Two interesting concepts are found in this phrase. The first is that the child will not learn the necessary lessons of life *overnight*. Quite often it is frustrating for the single parent, with a very limited amount of time, to have to constantly teach a child the same lessons. Just as soon as a parent feels that she can relax in a specific training area, her child shows that he has not yet learned the lesson.

"Becky knows that she must go to bed at 8:30 P.M., and yet all of a sudden she is testing me again on this issue. She cries and begs to stay up later, when I thought we were months beyond this sort of behavior." Becky's mother was finding out that Becky still needed her. This little girl was testing to find out if her mother was still interested in training her.

God, in his wisdom, knows that the training process for children takes many years. His statement is "When he is old, he will not depart from it." This is a warning to parents. Training is a long, drawn-out process with no instant answers.

The second lesson to be learned from this portion of the verse is the same lesson Moses had to learn. To say "and when he is old, he will not depart from it" gives a clear indication to the parent that when the child is young, he will not only depart from the training, but will likely resent the training and the trainer at times.

Many times the single parent will feel that her child is fighting her on every issue, so why should the parent bother? Why train the child when he acts as if he does not want to be trained? Children are not going to turn to a parent with a grateful heart and say, "Thank you for taking the time to structure my life, Mom."

The single parent is often looking for approval and support in her journey as a parent. When the trainer cannot find approval for

what she is doing for her children, she can
become discouraged. A parent cannot look to a
child for a thank-you for the job of training,
any more than Moses could turn to the Israelites. Moses finally had to learn to respond to
God. His encouragement came from the knowledge that he was doing what God wanted him
to do. The single parent must stop reacting to
the complaints of the child. Encouragement
must be found in the fact that God has commanded the parent to train the child. With this
command, God will supply the means to
accomplish the task. God never told Moses the
job would be easy, but he did give Moses the
ability to do his will. To which should a parent
respond: the command and encouragement of
God to train or the complaints and challenges
of the child to stop training?

The last part of Proverbs 22:6 is the promise
from God. As we train our child, when he is
mature or older, "he will not depart from it."
This promise can be either a great comfort and
encouragement or a frightening indicator of
the child's future. It is no coincidence that children who grow up in divorced families statisti-
cally stand a much greater chance of being
divorced themselves in later life. Many children have not been trained to be committed to

the marriage relationship. That accounts for why so many adults today have gotten divorced.

On the other hand, God has promised that if a parent takes the time to train a child the way God says he should be trained, then when he is old, he will not depart from that lesson. This encouraging promise from God is what every parent who is actively training wants to claim for her children. This is also the reason to train them in the way God would have them live.

God is promising here that if a parent is willing to make training a priority in the home, then when the child becomes older, he will remain true to the training. The parent's responsibility to train a child properly is awesome!

With these facts in mind, the single parent committed to training the child is now ready to begin the "Second Wilderness Journey." Now it is time to begin the uphill job of the day-to-day training of the child, the top-priority job that God has called the parent to do. To fail to accept the job is to allow the child to be trained and ruled by any taskmaster the world has to offer.

If Moses had not responded to God's command, the Israelites might have remained slaves in Egypt. If the single parent does not respond to the command of God to "train up the child," the child may never be able to break loose from the bondage of a life with little or no direction. The "Second Wilderness Journey"—that of training the child—is not any easier than the "First Wilderness Journey" discussed in Part One. It is, however, the command of God, and each parent who accepts his call to train her child will find the divine strength and wisdom to meet the challenge.

IN REVIEW
Principles of the Parental Calling
1. Single parents must be committed to train their children.
2. Single parents must accept the fact that training takes years.
3. Single parents must respond to God and not to the rebellion of the children.
4. Single parents can claim the promise that "he will not depart from it."

7

The Four *E*s of Training

In a seminar, I had just concluded the first-hour session on why a parent should train up a child. A distraught single mother came up to me during the break time to say, "I know that I am supposed to train my children. What I need is a plan. How does a parent go about training children?" In the remaining hours of the seminar this mother found the answer she needed. At the end of the retreat weekend she told me, "What helped me the most was the 'Four *E*s of Training.' That was a simple way to remember a plan for training that I can take home with me."

Before deciding *what* to train, a parent must

have a model showing her *how* to train. Most
parents know that they are expected to train.
They even have in mind many of the qualities
that they are supposed to instill in their children. In the case of the distraught mother at
the seminar, it was a matter of not knowing
how she as a trainer was supposed to get the
necessary lessons across to her children. Knowing what needs to be done and then how to do
it are two very different things.

No two children are alike, and family situations are different; but there are certain guidelines that can and should be followed. When I
first came to Sheridan House for Boys as their
new director, I quickly realized that my new
job entailed developing a relationship with
more than just people. There were also several
farm animals on the Sheridan House property.
This was a new experience for me, having
grown up in the city.

One weekend when the rest of the staff was
on vacation, I received a phone call from a
neighbor who informed me that one of our
cows was loose and out on the road. Having no
one qualified for the task, I got into our truck
and located the cow.

I knew what needed to be done. I had to
help that cow walk up into the back of the

truck. After I talked to the cow for a while and tried to nudge her into the truck, I began rougher tactics. I pulled from the front end and reluctantly pushed from the other end, all to no avail. Just then a man familiar with this sort of situation came walking over from his house. Without saying a word to "Bossy," he took a firm hold on one ear and another on the tail, and to my amazement that cow walked right up the ramp into the truck.

I had known what needed to be done, and that man (probably a farmer) had also known what needed to be done: the cow had to be put into the truck. The difference was that only one of us knew how to accomplish the task. He had a plan. The same is true for training children; parents need a plan. I recommend the "Four *E*s of Training a Child" plan.

PHASE ONE: EXAMPLE

The old adage that says, "Do as I say, not as I do," symbolizes the technique many single parents use in teaching their children. This approach, however, will not help a child learn anything of value. The first step in training a child is to be an example to the person who is to learn the lesson. Often a parent tries to train a child with long lectures and sporadic punishments.

"Are you ever going to learn to clean your room and make your bed? When will you grow up and accept some responsibility?" responded one parent to her child. When asked if she herself did what she was trying to teach her child to do, the mother replied, "I don't always have time as a single parent to clean my room." This may be partially true; however, if a parent is asking a child to "grow up and act like an adult" by performing certain tasks that she herself is not doing, then the child is being given mixed signals. What the parent wants to teach becomes a difficult lesson for the child to learn.

A child generally wants to appear as if he is acting like an adult. His parent is the role model, or example for the child to follow. Observing a parent helps him see just what being an adult is all about. What a parent does and the responsibilities that a parent accepts will demonstrate how to get a specific task done. It is interesting to me how many parents have sat in my office upset about the fact that their teenagers have recently been smoking cigarettes. Moments earlier many of these same parents had asked me for permission to smoke in my presence.

The parent must exhibit the behavior, sense of responsibility, and personal discipline for the child to see firsthand. For example, if a parent wanted to teach a child how to play baseball, he would not simply purchase a baseball, a glove, and a bat for his five year old and say, "There's the equipment, son. Now go have fun." No. The parent would take the child outside and say, "Sit down and watch while I show you the correct way to catch, throw, and bat." With this example to follow, the child could begin playing baseball the proper way. Being an example is the first step in training. That principle can be applied to other areas of child rearing. The chapters to follow will cover many of these important training topics.

An illustration of a more important nature will be of value here, however. Many single parents are concerned about teaching their children about sexual morality. A child may hear many lectures about the importance of sexual purity, but the most significant training tool will be the way the child's parent handles his or her own personal sexuality.

For single parents, the decisions and frustrations concerning sexual involvement out of wedlock are often very painful. The primary reason that a single person is to remain sexually pure is because of the commands of Jesus Christ. There is a second reason for the single parent: Children will follow the leadership of their parents. The example that a parent sets in being sexually pure will go a long way toward teaching a child about the importance of sexual purity. It goes without saying that the opposite is also true. If a single parent teaches her child that intercourse apart from the marriage relationship is wrong, but engages in such activity herself, she is making the lesson a difficult one to assimilate. The life-style a parent adopts is not only for her benefit, but also for her children's.

PHASE TWO: EXPOSURE

As a parent attempts to live a life that exemplifies what her child is to learn, the next step is to give the child guided exposure to the lessons. When my daughter reached the age of four, my wife and I decided that it was time for her to *begin* learning how to clean her room. For us the best time to accomplish this task was first thing each morning. We first established the fact that we were setting a good example in this area, and then my daughter, Torrey, and I started working in her room each morning. Torrey was not completely turned loose with the new responsibility. Instead she was helped with the new task, such as making her bed and straightening out her room. This phase of training for her merely *exposed* her to the lesson, with the trainer by her side. Together we performed the task. This stage of the training plan applies to almost every area of maturity or development for a child.

PHASE THREE: EXPERIENCE

Once a parent has exposed a child to different tasks or helped the child work on competence under close supervision, it is then time to move on to the third step. For many single parents this third stage is filled with anxiety. The prospect of letting one's child step out and do things on his own is sometimes frightening to the parent. This fear often hits for many different reasons.

Some single parents do not want to emancipate their children or allow them to feel that they can do things without "Mom's help." Many single parents subconsciously encourage their children to be dependent on them. With this

conscious or subconscious dependency relationship, the parent never allows or encourages the
child to "try his wings." He rarely gets the
opportunity to attempt by himself the things he
has been taught.

A second reason some single parents are
reluctant to let their children experience the
training lessons on their own is fear that the
child will fail. Their thought is often "If I just
help my child with this, he won't have to feel
unsuccessful." Unfortunately, the opposite is
also true. The child of an overprotective parent
will never have the opportunity to feel that he
has succeeded at anything without "Mom's
help." Whoever said that nothing can be learned
from our failures? If a child grows up in a home
where he is never allowed to fail, the adult world
is going to be a very difficult adjustment for
him. As a parent I prefer that my child experience both success and failure as a child while I
am available to help him cope, rather than have
him flounder as an adult.

The experience phase of the training process demands that the parent become an observer, rather than a participant, in the lesson
being taught. As one single parent put it,
"This is the most difficult part. I can get the
task at hand done so much more efficiently

and in half the time, that I have had to decide which was more important, the finished product or my daughter's development." The life of the single parent can be very hectic, and sometimes it is easier to do the job rather than to wait for the child to get it done.

In this third phase, however, the parent must decide that the child's growth is more important. By allowing the child to experience the task—by doing it and making the decisions about it himself—you are giving the child the opportunity to feel good about himself. This leads to the fourth and final phase of training— encouragement.

PHASE FOUR: ENCOURAGEMENT

When a child has completed a task or become accomplished in an area of responsibility, it is the job of the parent to give the child the proper feedback. This is often the stage that demands the most creativity on the parent's part. Because of the single parent's very busy schedule, this is also the stage that appears to be the least productive. That thought could not be further from the truth. Still, this positive stage is usually left out of the training process.

A job or an area of growth that is only partially accomplished or developed can be seen
from two directions. From one direction a
parent can see what is not completely accomplished or finished properly. The parent looking from this direction might feel justified in
reprimanding the child for not completing the
task. From the other direction, the parent
views what is completed and compliments the
child. The whole picture must be taken into
account.

An old tale illustrates this point. Two men
blind from birth were taken to the circus to
"see" an elephant. One went up front and felt
the trunk. He announced, "Now I know that
an elephant looks like a fire hose." "No, no!"
exclaimed the other blind man, as he stood
feeling the side of the animal. "An elephant
looks like the side of a house." Both men
were looking at the same animal, yet due to
their blindness they had two completely different views.

Do not be a blind parent. Take both angles
into account. When your child has attempted
to accomplish something you have trained
him to do, encourage him for what he has
accomplished. Then creatively show him how
to complete the remainder of the task.

Parent: "Robey, I appreciate your work on the lawn, son. The back yard looks great, and you did an excellent job getting up close to the trees. We could improve on this side lawn and you missed a spot by the curb. Let's go get the lawn mower and we'll finish it together."

Parent: "Torrey, your room looks much better. I like the way you have arranged the top of your dresser with all of those dolls. Why don't we fix the bed together and then work on the closet?"

Parent: "Barbara, you started this vacation doing a very good job of budgeting your own money, and I am proud of the way you kept track of what you spent. It appears that the day we spent in Atlanta was a hard one on your wallet. Let's take a look at how we can do better next time."

Many things were happening during these monologues. First of all, the children were encouraged and were made to feel that their accomplishments were important. They were shown what was done properly and encouraged for it, as well as how to improve in the areas that were unsatisfactory. Even though they were encouraged, the children were not permitted to think that they were totally successful in the task.

A second significant factor in these monologues is the parent's recognition that each child was in need of more help than was made available in the experience phase. Rather than simply observing the child redo or complete the task, the parent got actively involved in an effort to encourage the child further. Each time the parent dropped back to phase two and helped the child complete the training. The parent concluded by saying, "Let's do this together."

It was stated earlier, but is worth repeating: Though often overlooked by the single parent, this encouragement phase is extremely important. Without encouragement a child begins to think, *No one really cares when I take my time and do it correctly, so why should I?* Children need constant encouragement. Yet single parents with busy schedules often respond with a "crisis management approach." The parent responds only to problems and negative situations, rather than taking the time to balance the criticism with constructive encouragement. This fourth phase is much too often overlooked.

Where did these "Four *E*s of Training" come from? Not from the author of this book. They came from the Author of all creation. When Christ was on the earth, he was often referred to as a teacher (John 3:2). One of the ways that he used to train his disciples was by showing them how to live. They were able to observe the way he served others: "I have given you an example to follow" (John 13:15). Forgiving and loving others, Christ was the Example for his disciples to follow. He never said, "Do as I preach. Don't do as I do." Instead, Jesus set an example for all to follow.

Second, Jesus kept his disciples with him and allowed them to take part in his ministry. The disciples were called upon to help him feed the masses and give to the poor. Jesus exposed his followers to the Christian walk.

In Luke 9:2 Christ sent the disciples out on their own to minister to the needy. This was their opportunity to experience and attempt what they had been trained to do and then return to Christ with questions.

Last, Christ told his followers that the Holy Spirit would come after him to be the Encourager (Acts 1:8), and he himself encouraged his disciples in John 14. The Great Trainer created the plan for training. A parent need only follow this method in the areas in which the child needs to develop and grow.

IN REVIEW

The Four *E*s training plan can help a child achieve specific tasks and develop areas of maturity that he needs as he grows from infancy through adolescence.

1. *Example*–showing the child you practice what you preach.
2. *Exposure*–being a participant with the child in the lesson to be taught.
3. *Experience*–being an observer in the lesson being taught.
4. *Encouragement*–being an encourager as the child learns the lesson.

8

A Philosophy
of Life

"My children are fourteen and seventeen
years old, and they seem to make the worst
decisions. Both of them will do just about
whatever their friends want them to do, and
yet they've been raised to know better. I've
taken them to church most of their lives.
What's caused them to choose so many bad
paths to follow?"

This lament came from a single mother in
response to some undesirable behavior her
children were exhibiting. Many children in
today's world live "anchorless" lives, drifting

from decision to decision with no central philosophy to which to cling.

Donald Tucker, a psychologist in Boca Raton, Florida, who has studied children for years, notes that children must mature in eight areas before they reach adulthood. The most significant area that a child must be helped to develop for himself is a basic philosophy of life.

Just what is a philosophy of life? It is a core belief or motivator that helps a child make the decisions that he comes up against in life. Having a philosophy of life gives a child a pillar to cling to when new decisions or situations arise. If a child is making a moral decision, and has been developing a core philosophy, he can then measure a variety of possible decisions against his developing philosophy. His question to himself will be, "Does a yes to this decision go with or against what I believe?" The stronger the core belief, the greater the impact it will have on the decisions he makes. A philosophy of life will give him a measuring stick by which he can make life's decisions.

Often children from single-parent homes who are not trained in a proper philosophy of life develop their own self-centered, short-term beliefs. They may feel that life and especially adults cannot be depended upon because of broken promises or because they feel abandoned. All too often they may feel that tomorrow holds nothing worth waiting or working for; so why not life for today? This type of philosophy of life encourages the child to get what he can today because who knows what tomorrow might bring?

Some children from single-parent homes may be deterred from making bad decisions because they don't want to let their family down. Their philosophy of life does not permit them to hurt or to shame their family. On the other hand, many children from single-parent homes believe that other family members have already let the family down through the divorce. They no longer see their family structure or name as a worthy enough reason to deter them from bad decisions.

In today's fast-changing world, it is extremely important for children to develop a philosophy of life that is rooted in something more substantial and more consistent than mere human relationships.

In developing a core belief, each individual must choose one of three basic directions: material pursuits, people, or God. Deep down inside all of us, we have chosen to worship at one of these three basic altars of life.

Some people worship *material things*. Money and the acquisition of things that money can buy is one possible philosophy by which people make their life-changing decisions. This is a very tempting idol, especially to the single parent for whom finances are so often a major burden. The family's life-style has probably changed drastically, because the separation and the child support settlement have not worked out as expected. Hence, the single parent has had to go to work, and many of the bills are still not being paid.

In this situation, it does not take long before the stress brought on by insufficient funds causes many single parents to think, "If I only had more money, everything would be OK."

The decisions that these single parents make will probably revolve around becoming "secure" through more money. It might be better expressed by what Donna, a single mother once told me. "I began to think that I would be rescued from my lot in life by making more money. What I was doing was worshiping my paycheck." In coping with difficult times, this single mother had established a philosophy of life that treated money and material things as her god.

Donna soon began looking to a new god to

save her from her difficulties. She came to believe that instead of money, she should be worshiping people—more specifically, one individual. She felt that if she could just find a man who would marry her and help her with the children and finances, then everything would be wonderful. With this as her new core belief and main motivator, she was willing to do anything to make it happen. Unfortunately she ended up compromising herself with several men over the years. She easily justified her life-style, thinking it would help her to reach her goal of getting a husband and the security he would provide.

Donna is the same single mother who was wondering why her fourteen year old and seventeen year old were floundering so much morally. She had never really taken the time to step back and analyze her own attitude and actions. Without realizing it, she had been setting the wrong example for her children. God would have us adopt and teach our children a philosophy of life that enshrines neither things nor people. When Christ was cornered by the scribes, they basically asked him what the most important thing in life was (Mark 12:28-30). He replied by quoting Deuteronomy 6:4-5; "O Israel, listen: Jehovah is our God, Jehovah alone. You must love him with *all* your heart, soul, and might."

The philosophy of life that will help children to make better moral decisions is one that loves God and makes him the top-priority relationship in our life. Deuteronomy 6:6-7 further elaborates on this belief: "And you must think constantly about these commandments I am giving you today. You must teach them to your children and talk about them when you are at home or out for a walk; at bedtime and the first thing in the morning." If children have loving God and following his commandments as their philosophy of life, the decisions they will make in the future will be much less difficult. Training children to love Christ and his Word is the top-priority responsibility of parents, married or single.

PHASE ONE: EXAMPLE

In order to train a child to make Christ first in his life, the single parent must first make certain that Christ holds the top-priority position in his or her own life. Donna said that she took her children to church, but that falls far short of the job of training children to love Christ. First, Donna's priorities needed to be put in proper order. This single mother's life-style had to reflect the fact that she had recently made Christ the top priority of her life and looked up to him alone. Only Christ could save her from life's difficulties, as only Christ was to be worshiped and sought after. Donna had to be consistent in a philosophy of life that looked up to God, across to people as equals, and down at things. Material things were to be used; people were not.

How would Donna's life-style have to affect her children? They would have to see that their mother's new philosophy of life led her to spend time every day in prayer and Bible study, alone and with them. The children would have to be able to see clearly that this single mother's most important quest was getting closer to God and finding the path God had for her. The children would also have to sense that she held God's principles of life above all others.

Many Christians are able to talk "the Christian walk," but their lives do not display a genuine stand for God. Children are careful observers. They need to see that their parents not only truly believe what they say about God, but also are presenting a display or example for the children to follow.

"My mom took us to church and acted like

the rest of those Christians while we were there, but at home things were all back to normal," said Donna's oldest child. It reminded me of the father who took his son for a ride in the car to talk to his boy about the importance of honesty and obeying rules. Halfway through the conversation on honesty, the father reached down to turn on his "Fuzz Buster."

"It was as if an arrow had pierced my heart," the father later said. "Just as I turned the knob on the Fuzz Buster, my little boy asked me what it was for. The only true answer at this point in our lesson on the importance of honesty was that it was a device to help me be dishonest and break the law." When this father went home, he dismantled the Fuzz Buster. He realized that if his son were to learn how to follow the commandments of Christ and be an honest person, the boy would have to have a father whose life did not set a confusing example.

Training children in the importance of having Christ at the center of life means that single parents must first set the example.

PHASE TWO: EXPOSURE

Children should be exposed to Christian training as soon as possible. It can never be too early or too late. Personally, I was not exposed to Christian training until I was twenty-one years old. On the other hand, my children have been involved in our family devotions from such an early age that they will never be able to remember a time when we did not begin each day reading Bible stories.

Exposure to the Christian life means helping the child learn to have a regular devotional time. If this is truly the prevailing philosophy of life, then it should be important enough for the family to arrange their day so that a devotional time takes place. It can be a time of taking turns reading together as a family and praying out loud for each other. In our home, it includes a song every day. Children learn much from singing. I'm sure that if anyone walked by our home at 6:30 A.M. and heard the Barnes' break out in song, they might, in turn, pray for our sanity. This, however, has become a very special time for us. For any family it will be a positive way to send the children off into the day.

A family can also keep a prayer request journal. In this log of prayers, the children can participate in writing down prayer requests and dating them. It is always an enriching experience to go back to this log later and see how many prayers (especially the ones that everyone had forgotten about) have been answered.

There are many decisions about life, involvement in church activities, and the handling of friends that parent and child can discuss together. During these times they can relate Christian values to the child's daily life; for example, "How would a Christian treat a friend who has hurt him?" could spark much fruitful discussion. A single parent can help a child see the priority that activities at church should take. Through regular exposure to Christian values at home, the child can begin making decisions on his own.

PHASE THREE: EXPERIENCE

This is a highly significant and also frightening stage in the development of a philosophy of life. Children must have the awesome opportunity to develop their own relationship with God and their own philosophy, rather than simply look to their parents. They also need the opportunity to experience their own devotional life. The frightening aspect is related to their having to make some of their own decisions about life while they are still at home. The chance to test their philosophy of life is crucial for their future, when they leave the nest.

If a child exposed to church-related activities and Christ-honoring decisions has been fairly successful in these parent-guided experiences, it may be time for him to make some of his own decisions. At age sixteen one child had a new revelation when she told her mother, "I'd rather not go to youth choir practice tonight. I've been to all the others. Can I stay home?"

Her mother responded, "If you feel that you have a reason that God would honor, you can stay home."

"Don't *you* want to know why?" the girl asked.

"No, tonight's decision is between you and God" was the single mother's reply. This wise mother was helping her daughter learn that she was really responsible to God above all others.

This was a new and awesome responsibility for the daughter, who said, "For the first time in my life I realized that I wasn't doing things just to please Mom. Activities like choir became a new chance for me to please and praise God."

This young girl did not march right out

from that day on and make great decisions in all of life's situations. There were often times of reevaluation between her and her mother. One time in the area of decisions about dating, it became obvious that this girl's Christian philosophy of life was not prevailing. Mother and daughter needed to go back to making decisions together; so they returned to the exposure phase for a period of time.

The experience phase, with all its anxieties and failures, is a very tenuous time for the single parent. It is difficult to be in the position of leadership alone and begin allowing the child some freedom in these decisions. For a child to grow and develop, however, a philosophy of life must become his very own. He must have the opportunity of failure and growth. An important ingredient for this growth is encouragement.

PHASE FOUR: ENCOURAGEMENT

Many times a child will not receive much feedback from his peers for his faith and the decisions that coincide with his faith. A single parent must be on the alert to encourage these difficult decisions whenever they arise. Children will often feel an aloneness about their decisions. This is an emotion that the single parent can easily identify with herself. Sharing with the child about these feelings of loneliness is invaluable.

At times church activities will conflict with plans that the child's friends have. If he agonizingly decides to go to church for youth choir practice rather than to go out with his friends, he should be encouraged.

Parent: "I know you were having a difficult time deciding what to do about youth choir Friday night, Bill. I'm proud of you for putting your responsibilities over and above pleasure. You are really growing up."

Parent: "I was almost moved to tears when I walked by your room last night and saw that you were having your devotions. It is reassuring to me to know that you, too, are praying for our family. Thank you."

Remember that children will not be saints. The parent in the example above could have just as truthfully stated, "It's about time you read your Bible. I haven't seen you pick that book up in weeks." Instead, she chose to encourage the positive behavior. All children, regardless of their family situation, are going to make some poor decisions. Developing a philosophy of life, however, helps them begin to make more and more consistent decisions. As the promise in Proverbs 22:6 says, "When he is old, he will not depart from it" (KJV).

A single parent can make use of many other tools to instill an overall, long-term philosophy of life. This closing example illustrates the effects of using a plan to train your child.

A woman I know quite well had a very firm conviction that, as a mother, one of her priorities was to train her four children about the love of Christ. She decided that before her children grew up and left home, they would be trained about what it meant to have a strong faith in God as their overall philosophy of life. To set a firm example, this mother developed her own personal faith to help the children see what her priority was: to love Christ and serve him. She exposed the four children at an early age to family devotions, and many mornings the children would try to avoid the family time with God. They often tested their mother to see if these devotions were truly important to her. Never once did a child say, "Thank you, Mom. That Bible story you read this morning was great." This mother was not responding to reinforcement from the children, however; she was responding to God.

As the children grew into adolescence, they were allowed to make many decisions on their own. The three boys were not angels and frequently made very poor decisions. The improper decisions were dealt with, and the good decisions were encouraged and reinforced. The key to this training, however, is that the mother did not quit the spiritual training simply because the children did not respond positively.

Many years later, the family was together at Christmas time, and the middle son made the statement, "You know, Mom, now that I have children of my own, one of the things that I appreciate most about the way you raised us was that we could always count on having devotions every morning no matter where we were."

This mother could barely contain her tears because it was the first time she had ever received any positive feedback from one of her children about their devotional time. She had known the importance of living out a strong philosophy of life for her children. Instead of responding to the children's seeming disregard, she had responded to God.

Today this mother's daughter, Rosemary, is in the ministry with me as my wife and greatest spiritual adviser. And what about those three boys? Peyton, the youngest, is a Presbyterian minister; Slade is a Southern Baptist minister, and Arlo works for a Christian company. Yes, there were the normal hard times during the adolescent years, but each of these children was able to develop a philosophy of life that has helped him find direction. This is due, at least in part, to a parent who saw the need to be consistent in the training plan for her four children.

In this rapidly changing world a child needs an anchor that will keep him from straying too far. That anchor is a core belief of who he is and whose he is (God's). This will help him have a consistent guideline for the numerous decisions he must make. Faith in Christ is the only philosophy of life that a child can count on to carry him through life.

IN REVIEW
Principles for Instilling a Philosophy of Life
1. EXAMPLE
    The life-style of the single parent must show that the priorities are:
    God first
    People second
    Things third.

2. EXPOSURE

Family life must include activities that allow for Christian growth:

Family devotions
Family prayer
Worship.

3. EXPERIENCE

Children should be allowed opportunities to make decisions about their lives.

4. ENCOURAGEMENT

Single parents must not forget to take the time to praise children for making wise Christian decisions.

HITTING HOME

What is your plan as a single parent to help your child develop a philosophy of life?

1. What things in my life truly show that Christ is my top priority?

a. _____

b. _____

c. _____

2. What regular activities in my home help my child grow closer to Christ?

a. _____

b. _____

c. _____

3. What opportunities to make his own Christian decisions have I given my child recently?

a. _____

b. _____

c. _____

4. What was the last thing I praised my child for concerning his spiritual growth? Concerning anything?

a. _____

b. _____

c. _____

9

Self-Esteem

"My teenager sometimes acts as if he would
like to have fun with our family again. But
just as he begins to let himself go, something
seems to stop him. It is almost as if he looks
into an imaginary mirror, sees himself having
fun, and quits because he feels unworthy of
enjoying his family."

This statement from a single parent sums up
why many children withdraw from their families. It reflects probably the most profound
area of difficulty in the single-parent home:
the self-esteem of the child.

"My parents got divorced because of me" was the explanation a fourteen-year-old boy gave me at Sheridan House.

"How old were you when they got divorced?" I asked him.

"I'm not sure," the boy replied. "I think I was about a year and a half old."

Once again I asked, "What's made you think that you were the cause of the divorce?"

The child's response to this question startled me, but I have since come to know that it is not an uncommon thought for children of divorce. He said, "I don't really know why I feel like I caused the divorce. No one has ever told me why my mom and dad broke up. Over the years I have figured that it just must have been my fault."

To some, the child's response might seem very unrealistic. To this young boy with a low self-esteem, however, it made a great deal of sense. His parents, though not living together, had given all the indications that they felt fine about themselves. They gave no real explanation for the divorce or at least no explanation that the child could accept or understand.

Left to his own reasoning, this child decided over a period of years that his parents were both adults and thus did not have all the problems that a child has. It did not take long for him to begin to surmise that he must have been the weak link. They must have been happy until he came along. This child was all too familiar with his own inadequacies. His very low self-esteem convinced him that as an infant, he must have been capable of doing something to cause the marriage to break up. A child with low self-esteem can make himself believe that he is somehow the cause of almost any of the family's mishaps.

Quite possibly a child, from time to time, may hear his parents arguing about him and the way he is being raised or disciplined. Such arguing may be only the outward manifestation of deeper problems between the two adults. The child may not know how deep the problems are between his parents, but only that he has witnessed himself as the cause of the conflict between them. As the outward marital conflicts continue and divorce takes place, a child can come to feel as if he was at least one of the causes of the break-up.

What is self-esteem? Psychologists tell us that self-esteem is the attitude a person has about his own values, his goals, his abilities, and his own personal worth. Self-esteem has a great impact on the way a person feels about himself. His decision about how he views himself will affect his relationship with other people and the world around him. Self-esteem has an influence on the friends a person will choose, as well as the choice a person makes for a spouse. The way one feels about himself affects myriad things in his life, not the least of which is the way he responds or fails to respond to his family.

A child in a single-parent home may not feel as if he played a significant part in causing the divorce, and yet he may still withdraw from the family due to a poor feeling about himself. Self-esteem is an attitude cultivated initially and primarily by the family unit. A family that has had a major disruption may have also disrupted the development of the child's self-esteem.

EARLY CHILDHOOD

The process of helping a child form a positive image of himself begins at birth. There are three basic aspects of this development in the life of an infant. The first of these aspects is the way the infant perceives that his *physical needs* are met. These include hunger, warmth, and comfort (such as a dry diaper). This is the most primary of care. Often, however, families are in such turmoil that mostly just the basic needs are all that are being met.

A second aspect of self-esteem development for the infant could be labeled *emotional needs.* Under this category would come genuine affection, cuddling, and reassurance. With his emotional needs being met, an infant can begin to feel that he is loved and wanted, rather than being a bother to his parents. No wonder children who are abused by a parent suffer such deep emotional scars. They have an intense need to feel loved and wanted, yet the parent may give them the opposite message. Meeting an infant's emotional needs makes him feel special. When a young child feels special, he is much more excited about taking advantage of his third need and that is the need for *sensory stimulation.*

Sensory stimulation is giving an infant the opportunity to explore his world by touch, taste, smell, hearing, and sight. As a child begins to feel good about himself, he is motivated to risk trying new things on his own, such as walking and communicating. Failure is not such a frightening prospect because he feels loved and cherished.

A single parent can give a small child a

sense of worth by listening to the child as he attempts to communicate. When a parent listens, it shows that she respects the child. Many times it is during the infancy stage of life that the marriage turmoil takes place. The parents are a child's security. If they are fighting and dealing with their marital problems, it may leave them little time for listening as the child tries to communicate. This situation can be overcome if the single parent will once again become the child's number-one fan.

An infant goes through many developmental stages. As he conquers each one, he looks to his parent for approval. A parent may cheer when he walks or uses the potty or eats his peas. In doing this, the parent becomes president of the child's own personal fan club. No matter when the divorce takes place, there is going to be a period of time surrounding the divorce process when the child will lose the attention of his greatest fan or fans. Due to emotional drain and conflict, the parent is not as available as she once was to offer praise to the child.

To an adult this situation is understandable. After all, the divorce is a very difficult time, and it is all the parent can do to meet her own needs. The trauma of the divorce would natu-

rally preoccupy the parents for a while. It is
not logical or understandable to the child, however. It is extremely difficult for the child to
lose his encouragers at such an unstable time
in the life of the family.

The parents need to remember that they are
not the only family members going through
the divorce. The child is also trying to sort
things out and understand why he is being
abandoned. He could feel abandoned physically
by the noncustodial parent and emotionally by
the single parent that remains at home. This is
a time when the fan club should be at its
strongest, but the trauma that the custodial
parent is dealing with makes this impossible.
As she gets her feet back on the ground however, the fan club can resume its cheering and
encouragement of the child in his conquest of
his environment.

When Mom starts cheering again about the
fact that Tommy can ride a three-wheeler, then
Tommy can feel that he has a right to feel good
about himself: "Mom thinks I'm special, so I
must be."

A single parent can also help a young child
experience a sense of confidence by establishing rules and structure in the home. As
a child learns to obey the rules, he can begin

to feel another sense of mastery over his environment. When there are well-explained, consistent rules in a home, a child has the opportunity to know when he is doing the right thing and when he is not. Discipline, structure, and consistency do much to help a child in his struggle for stability.

The single-parent home may often seem to the child like a leaky ship pumping bilge water. It is not quite sinking anymore, but it is also not yet seaworthy and stable. A home with no structure and rules can give a child a feeling of instability. As the single parent takes the time to consistently enforce the rules and maintain healthy structure, the child will be made to feel that the family is once again out of deep water. The child will have a sense of confidence in his family and its single-parent leadership. This confidence will allow the young child to begin to feel better about himself.

More will be said about the importance of discipline in chapter 14, but one quick word about healthy structure can be added here. Healthy structure exists when the rules are consistent enough for the child to understand, but not so rigid that he cannot have the free-dom to play and explore his environment. He must be allowed to be a child.

ELEMENTARY SCHOOL YEARS

The single parent can be established or rees-
tablished in the role of the child's fan and
encourager during the early childhood years.
As the child enters the elementary school
years, he will find that he must deal with new
people on a regular basis. His personality or
role is defined not only by the people at home,
but also by people outside the family. School-
mates, playmates, and teachers help the child
see who he is and where he fits.

Dorothy Corkville Briggs, in her excellent
book *Your Child's Self-esteem,* describes these
new significant people in the child's life as "mirrors." Just as the single parent acted as a mirror
by helping the child see who he is, the new playmates and classmates do the same. As a child
interacts with another individual, he gets a
sense of who he is by the response or reflection
he receives from another individual. The mirror
can be very encouraging or oftentimes overly
cruel. The new mirrors with which the elementary school child comes in contact are often not
very encouraging. They rarely become fan club
members, since they themselves are also struggling to develop their own sense of worth.

The elementary school years are the

beginning of socialization for the child. He quickly comes to realize that he is not the only six year old who wants to eat first, sit next to the teacher, and so on. Once again the task of the single parent is to be a fan and an encourager while helping the child with opportunities to develop the skills he needs at this age. His self-esteem will be affected by people outside the family from this point of his life on. As his single-parent family settles down into a routine that is consistent and nurturing, he can stop worrying about its stability and face the new challenges at hand.

The task in front of him is twofold: acceptance from his peers and the mastery of physical, social, and academic skills. These two areas often go hand in hand. As most children gain confidence in one of these areas, they are willing to try harder in the other. Unfortunately, the inverse can also be true. If a child arrives at school from a home filled with turmoil and instability, he has not been properly prepared to launch out into the new challenges at school. The child brings his emotional insecurities to the classroom and may find it difficult to make new friends. Thus feeling more insecure and unwanted, he cannot concentrate on developing his new academic skills.

The single parent can help the child develop the social skills necessary to the growth of his self-esteem by encouraging the child to join constructive groups of other children. Scouts, Sunday school, church choirs, athletic teams, ballet classes, and many other group activities are available. There are many things to look for when selecting a church to attend. "Does the church minister to the child with various constructive activities?" is an all-important question to ask.

When a group or activity has been selected, the single parent must show how important it is by actively supporting both the child and the group. For a single parent to simply drop the child off and never participate or observe makes a statement to the child. Children know that a single parent's most limited resource is not the money for the ballet lessons, but the time the parent spends watching. Time given by the single parent endorses the child and the activity in which the child is involved. The endorsement helps build the child's feelings of personal significance and self-esteem.

It is also important to make the home available to the child's friends. If a child is to feel good about his family, he should be able to invite friends over to play or to spend the night. He must feel comfortable about bringing his new friends into his old safe environment. Developing new relationships is important to his growth. A child should be given responsibilities, but not so many that he has no time to be with his friends.

A multitude of ingredients in a child's environment go into the building of his self-esteem. Conversely, the child's self-esteem has an obvious impact on the way he deals with his environment. The two are intricately interwoven. When he looks into the faces and examines the responses of those around him, he tries to perceive the image of himself that they as mirrors reflect. He will make many decisions according to the reflection he perceives. Should he try to befriend this child or that child? Should he raise his hand in class or just keep quiet? The role of the single parent must be to continue as his fan and encourager. A totally accepting fan will make a child feel that he always has someone to fall back on during difficult periods of development.

As the single parent encourages the young child to join the various activities available, she must also realize the all-important step that she is endorsing. The single parent is really encouraging the child to develop competencies outside the home. To become more independent, he is beginning his emancipation from the home and from her. It will be many years in coming, but emancipation is much more successful if it is taken in short steps over many years. If a child is isolated from others and remains dependent on Mom for feedback, going out into the world at eighteen can be a frightening experience.

Regardless of the single parent's own personal needs, the most healthy thing is to allow the child to feel better and better about his ability to cope with the activities of the outside world. It will help the child and the single parent when the time eventually arrives to cut the emotional apron strings. Ultimately, self-esteem is measured by the way a child feels he is valued as an individual, apart from the family. Then he can contribute himself and his abilities back to his family.

ADOLESCENCE

The experience of puberty and middle school bring along significant opportunities to test the child's self-esteem. Adolescence forces a child to stand as an individual. His school is bigger, and each class has different individuals rather than the same students all day long. The adolescent now spends more time away from home than ever before in his life, and his main focus of development is to find out who he is as an individual.

The single parent's role should be to show her commitment to the family and to the teenager. This can appear to be an unfulfilling task because the teenager is at an age when he is giving conflicting messages. Though he wants and needs a strong family to come home to for emotional support, his inclination at this age is toward independence from the family. Without the support of a partner, the single parent can become very confused. One parent put it this way:

> "I don't know whether I'm wasting my time or not. I set up a family picnic and my teenager backs out at the last minute. I know she doesn't have anything better to do, but it seems like the mere mention of doing something as a family turns her off."

The conflicting messages of the teenager can be very unnerving. Often he is saying, "I do want to go, but I am not sure I belong."

He may not even know that this is what he is feeling. He may not know that he really wants his parent to say, "This is still a family, and when we go places as a family we *need* you along." At times a teenager may feel more acceptance from peers and thus may want to be with them. He avoids being with the family partially because he feels inadequate.

Linda Bird Francke in *Growing Up Divorced* writes about this age and its mood changes as a time that keeps the single parent constantly off balance. A single parent who is relying on the teenager's responses for encouragement will eventually give up. As the child enters these final phases of developing his self-esteem, he will be testing the skills he has been taught. When a sixteen year old makes some money other than his allowance, he will be testing his skill at economics. Everything he has been taught comes into play during this age. He is also establishing his independence from family and even peers to eventually become an individual.

Just as the child needed a fan club when he took his very first step, so, too, the teenager needs his parent's encouragement. The single parent must be alert for opportunities to encourage him.

The plan is still the same. The single parent must allow the child room to grow, even as he is away from the family. The home must still be a place where he is special, however.

As the teenager is out there battling for recognition like everyone else, he will often come home with his emotions and confidence bruised. It is a wise parent who makes the home a haven for him to return to and find encouragement. Rarely if ever will the teenager say, "Thank you" or "That was a great time we had today, Mom." The single parent must continue being the child's *unconditional* fan because it is necessary, not because it is acknowledged.

Children of all ages—from toddlers to teenagers—must feel that they are loved for who they are and not for what they have accomplished. In order for a child to feel secure and have an opportunity to develop his own self-esteem, he must feel that the love he receives from his parent is an unconditional, totally accepting love. Often children test this in very strange and unconscious ways.

I wish I had counted how many single parents have asked me why their child began wetting the bed again at seven or eight years old. Many times after divorce or separation, a child gropes for a more secure environment. In my opinion, the child in the single-parent home may unconsciously "ask" for the opportunity to revert back to a developmental stage in which he felt more secure. The child will not literally ask. Instead he will exhibit the characteristics of an earlier developmental stage.

A five year old may ask if he can once again use a bottle with a nipple or go back to sucking his thumb. Another child may go back to crawling or act afraid of the dark and want to sleep in Mommy's bed. Still other children may wet the bed after having been potty trained for years. In order for the child of the single-parent home to develop a healthy self-esteem, he must be allowed to have the feeling that he can grow at his own speed, even if it means going momentarily backward.

Too many teenagers in single-parent homes are also thrust into burdensome adult roles. The lonely parent may turn to the fourteen year old for camaraderie in the grief. Rather than assuming the leadership, the single parent actually leans on the teenager for support. In this situation the child can be forced into adulthood too quickly. There is not the necessary freedom for the child to grow and develop at a comfortable rate.

Each growth step a child takes forces him to leave behind things that are familiar. The child should know that he has the freedom to venture back to previous stages every now and then when he feels insecure. If he knows he can do this and if the single parent does not try to force him into the harsh realities of adulthood before he is ready, then he can proceed with confidence—confidence in the feeling that he is free to go at his own pace.

Self-esteem is a feeling that is first nurtured in the home. If the single parent cherishes the child for who he is, rather than for what he has or has not accomplished, the child will continue to develop. A child must know that his worth is not based on beauty, accomplishment, or appropriate behavior. When a child knows that he is cherished at home and that his parent is his unfailing fan, he will reach out and try new things. He will have the confidence that he can always return home to a safe, loving atmosphere. Knowing that he can retreat without a feeling of dishonor will encourage a child to strike out on his own.

Self-esteem is measured by the child as he decides what the significant others in his life think about him. Though a single parent may not always believe it, no one is more significant in the preadolescent's and the teenager's life than the custodial parent.

IN REVIEW
Principles in Developing Self-Esteem
1. A child initially learns who he is by the way the single parent responds to him.
2. The single parent is the "mirror" he looks into to see if he is a valuable person.
3. In the single-parent home, it is the job of the custodial parent to work overtime to assure the child he is cherished for who he is and not for what he can do.
4. The single parent must become the child's number-one fan, praising him and encouraging him from infancy on through the difficult teenage years.
5. The single parent is a very powerful influence on the development of the child's self-esteem.

HITTING HOME
What is your plan to help your child develop a positive, healthy self-esteem?

1. When in recent times, did I arrange my schedule so that I was able to spend time observing my child in some activity?

    a. _____

    b. _____

    c. _____

2. What things do I do or say to help my child feel special?

    a. _____

    b. _____

    c. _____

3. What activities do I encourage my child to get involved in?

    a. _____

    b. _____

    c. _____

10

Communication

"My child and I don't communicate with each other. We seem to growl instead."

"My child is only three, but when do we begin to communicate in a way which will last?"

What do both those statements reveal? A lack of basic understanding of what communication is all about. Constructive, caring conversation between two people is only one of many forms of communication. In previous pages of this book the need for this kind of communication was mentioned as a necessary tool in the training plan. One mother's response summed it all up.

"That's all fine," she said, "but how do I get my child to start talking to me?"

Many people think that there is a special age at which communication begins and the child sits down and talks. For better or for worse, however, communication between parent and child begins almost at birth.

An infant has basic needs that he immediately learns to communicate to the parent: avoidance of physical discomfort (hunger, wetness, coldness, pain, and so on), craving for love and attention. The mode of communication used by the infant is crying until the needs are met. The parent in turn communicates to the infant by the way in which she or he responds to the child.

One single parent may pick up a crying infant and do more than just meet a basic need. By extra cuddling and talking to the infant, warmth and love are communicated. Another single parent, pressed for time by an overly busy schedule, may do no more than meet the bare essentials of care. She is communicating to the infant that he is just one more object on the long list of things to be done.

Single parents with infants may be going through a very difficult emotional time. While not meaning to, they could communicate to the infant that the one pillar of security he has—the single parent herself—cannot always be relied upon.

Another difficulty regarding communication in the single-parent home may be the lack of vital communication skills. Such a lack on the part of the single parent and noncustodial parent might have been a major factor leading to the divorce itself. Now the single parent finds herself wanting to communicate with her child, but not being sure how to do it. Frustration often causes the single parent to lecture and shout as the means of communication. Some children have spent time in a home where Mom and Dad fought or even screamed at each other before the divorce. In the new single-parent home where the mother often resorts to screaming, the child will also learn to scream as his mode of communication. The child can also begin to think that it is better just to tell his mother what she would like to hear, even if it is not true. Doing that helps avoid arguments.

Lack of the necessary communication skills is not the only enemy to positive communication. Many single parents either appear to be or make themselves too busy to share their feelings with their children. On the surface such sharing seems too unproductive, especially when the dishes are sitting there waiting to be washed. Eventually the child learns that there is no two-way communication, just short lectures from his mother. As the single parent continually dominates the conversation, it does not take long for the child to just give up. Instead of trying to express a feeling, the child simply waits for the sermon to be over.

Another big enemy to communication in the home is television. The excuse is often made that there are not enough hours in the day to do all that is necessary, and yet families can find several hours daily to spend in front of a television. In the single-parent home the television has become a baby-sitter. A child in today's society can spend time receiving information and stimuli from television programs, while spending no time responding or expressing opinions. Due to the time it robs, and the one line of communication (receiving only) that it teaches, television is a hindrance to genuine family communication.

The biggest deterrent to communication in the single-parent home, however, is often caused by the way the single parent herself deals with her grief. Divorce may have relieved the strain, but there is still a sense of loss on

the part of both parent and child. The family
typically has also experienced a loss in income.
The single parent's response to the situation
quite often is to throw herself into the job of
supporting the family and running the home.
By doing this, she avoids facing her grief. This
grief, however, must be faced and allowed to be
worked through by the single parent. Generally, though, she tries to keep busy to avoid
dealing with the pain.

The child, on the other hand, quite often
has dreams of getting his parents back
together. He forgets the difficulties during the
marriage and now fantasizes about how he can
be the matchmaker that restores the family.
Real communication between single parent
and child will reveal these two very different
sets of feelings. Many times the single parent
avoids in-depth communication with the child
in order to avoid having to face the grief and
her child's impossible dreams.

When no communication takes place, many
children never learn how to give verbal expression to their feelings. Like the infant who
sends messages by crying, some children never
move beyond the stage that Drs. Paul Ackerman and Murray Kappelman call "signals." In
their book *Signals,* Ackerman and Kappelman

discuss the various nonverbal messages that children send to their parents: frustration, hurt, fear, and other feelings.

When a child has learned the skill of verbalizing these emotions and he has a listening parent, much can be done to help the child deal with his feelings. But when a child has not been taught communication skills, the single parent must interpret the signals. Just as with a nontalking baby who is crying in the night, the parent must spend extra time interpreting the signal before the child can be helped. Eventually, as the parent goes down the imaginary checklist of possibilities, the problem is discovered.

With a child who does not verbally communicate hurt or loss, the single parent must go through even more frustration. The child's behavior or moodiness has to be analyzed and interpreted because when this child is asked, "What's the matter, Son?" his typical response will be "Nothing."

It must be added here that all children will give signals to some extent. However, the more adept a child is at communication skills and the more willing the single parent is to listen, the less need the child will have for signals.

In the single-parent home when signals are

used to communicate, they usually build in intensity and turn into more negative behavior. The initial signals take the parent too much time to interpret. Nothing is usually done about these initial signals; so they grow to a crisis proportion. At this point, the single parent usually tries to communicate verbally with the child. Unfortunately, past experiences have made the child feel as if communication is a waste of time. He thinks he does not really know how to say what he feels anyway. Developing positive communication skills in a family takes an investment of time and a willingness to listen.

PHASE ONE: EXAMPLE

A child will learn how to communicate much the same way he learns other skills: by watching and imitating a parent. The single parent must be willing to dedicate valuable time to communication. Once time is allotted, the key ingredient is to be an active listener. Francis of Assisi has been credited with a prayer that shows he truly understood what active listening is: "Lord, grant that I may seek more to understand than to be understood."

Listening to a child means that the single

parent must try to put her own concerns aside in order to understand what the child is trying to say. The adult listener should use more than just ears as the child talks. Eye contact and often physical cues can show a child that the single parent is really listening. When the child wants to discuss a problem or a concern, the single parent must not continue watching television or reading the paper. So often, a time-conscious single parent tries to do two things at once: listening while writing a grocery list. Other times she is not really listening, but just waiting for her own turn to talk.

How often all of us do that! Instead of truly listening and concentrating on what is being said, we concentrate on what we want to say next. I might have no idea what you were really trying to tell me, but I am certainly prepared to say what I want to say. That is not listening. It is simply being quiet. When the single parent sets that kind of communication example, she is encouraging the child to abandon verbal communication and return to signals. When this happens, it generally does not take long before both single parent and child become so frustrated that they oscillate between silence and screaming.

The single parent must show the child that she is willing to take time to communicate.

Then she should exhibit the characteristics of active listening so that the child experiences the joy of being listened to. With this example, the child will learn how to communicate, and at the same time he will be made to feel that his opinion is important.

PHASE TWO: EXPOSURE

In-depth communication at a level that expresses feelings takes time to develop. As the single parent herself desires to communicate at a feeling level, it will help the child. John Powell, in his book *Why Am I Afraid to Tell You Who I Am?* says that we communicate on at least five levels.

The fifth level is very safe and shallow, and is labeled *cliché communication*. Imagine a child walking into the kitchen in the morning. The dialogue might go like this:

Parent: "Good morning."
Child: "Good morning."
Parent: "Did you have a good rest?"
Child: "Yes."

Nothing is really said in this kind of communication, which is little more than acknowledging that the person has walked into the room. Another classic example of cliché communication happens every day after school.

Parent: "How was school today, Son?"
Child: "Fine."

The fourth level of communication takes place when the single parent and the child talk and simply report facts about other people.

Parent: "I saw Johnny with a new bike yesterday."
Child: "He just got it for his birthday."

This is still a very safe form of communication, because it keeps the topic away from anything personal. Nothing more than facts are reported, and so there is really nothing gained by this communication as far as the parent-child relationship is concerned.

The next level toward quality communication is where the single parent and the child begin to express ideas and judgments. In this third level of communication the person is beginning to risk taking a step closer toward revealing his or her feelings.

Parent: "A mother's place is to be home with the children, not working two jobs."
Child: "Maybe I should get a job after school to help with the bills."

Feelings are just barely approached at this level. They are not yet completely verbalized, but the feelings can be seen between the lines. This is perhaps the level of communication that takes place in most homes.

Level number two is when the single parent and the child begin to express emotions. The feelings that are verbalized are about facts or things rather than about their relationship.

Parent: "You know, Son, it depresses me to get into that old car and try to drive it around town."
Child: "I never told you this before, but I am embarrassed when you drive me to school in it."

Feelings and emotions are being expressed at this level, but they are directed toward objects.

The level-one form of communication is one in which the single parent and the child feel that they can be completely open with each other. In this type of relationship a child can express a hurt or an opinion without fear of reprisal from the single parent. In order for the child to begin expressing his in-depth feelings, his parent must be willing to initiate this kind of communication.

Parent: "The other day when you said that you had the greatest time at your dad's [or mom's] new house, I must confess that I was really hurt. I want you to have a good time when you're with your dad [mom], but it still hurt."

Thirteen-year-old Child: "I'm sorry my statement hurt you, Mom [Dad], but I do want you to know how I feel. Should I try to be more sensitive and stop telling you about my weekends with Dad [Mom]? I don't want to hurt you."

Parent: "No. You should be able to tell me those things. I'll just have to work on my feelings about your weekends away. I love you so much, and I guess sometimes I feel a little insecure about your love for me even though you haven't given me any reason to feel insecure."

Communication of this type builds quality relationships. Here the single parent and the child have worked to the point where they feel they can trust each other with their feelings. They are confident that when one reveals himself to the other, the information will not be used or manipulated by the other person.

H. Norman Wright has done an excellent job of discussing these areas of communication in his book *Communication: Key to Your Marriage.* The overall communication skills offered in Wright's book add another facet to this subject.

In today's world, a person can take out his appointment book and find that he has penciled in appointments for haircuts, work on the car, and many other "important" things. Yet so often we do not schedule time for our children.

A child needs opportunities to be exposed to quality communication so that he can begin learning how to assume his rightful place in the family and community. One way to ensure that the opportunity is available is for the single parent to go out on "dates" alone with the child.

With the busy life of a single parent, it is a must to schedule special time with the child. If not, the child ends up getting whatever parts of the day or week happen to be left over. These left-over times usually occur when the single parent is the most exhausted and thus too tired to truly communicate.

Making a special date with the child to go out to lunch together is one possibility. When the child and his single parent leave the every-day surroundings on regularly scheduled times, the stage is set for both parties to communicate. This communication time is not an outing to the movies or some other form of entertainment. It should be a time when parent and child are alone together with only a mild distraction such as eating or shopping. The mild distraction helps to take some of the pressure off the child as he attempts to communicate. It is during these "dates" that the single parent should practice listening and show the child that his opinion is being sought. The conversation should include phrases that evoke feelings.

Parent: "How did you feel when Michael broke your model airplane?" *or* "How did you feel when you and Laurie were arguing?"

A child needs to be taught to express feelings rather than just report facts.

Many people will say here that they just do

not have this kind of time. I read somewhere
once that the mother of Charles and John
Wesley had seventeen other children. She lived
at a time when there were none of the conve-
niences that we have today. The beautiful thing
is that Mrs. Wesley spent one hour a week
alone with each child. That is a total of nineteen hours each week. It was probably very difficult for her, and it is easy to imagine that she
must have made great personal sacrifices in
order to spend that amount of time. One-on-
one communication must have meant a great
deal to her.

In generations past, prior to the arrival of
schedules that pulled everyone away from the
home and before the invention of the television, families used to spend time around the
dinner table. Eating the evening meal was only
part of the reason families gathered around the
table together. They were also there to talk and
get to know and love each other. People did
not eat and run, thus distancing themselves
from family interaction.

Today the single parent can encourage communication by once again using the dinner
hour for more than eating. Unfortunately, in
many single-parent homes the family may not
even eat at the same time. If the parent takes

the initiative to encourage the children back to the table, it can be the start of a special time for the family.

To help keep the children at the table at Sheridan House for Youth we have from time to time initiated dinner games. We want the boys to get into the habit of remaining at the table after meals.

One such game used in my home while I was growing up was the alphabet game. First, a topic is chosen: automobiles, animals, cities, and so on. Then the game moves around the table as each person takes a turn thinking of something on the topic that starts with the next letter of the alphabet. The purpose of the game is not to think of the topic, however; it is to get children back to the table. As time goes on, remaining at the table becomes a habit, and the conversation can gradually become more in-depth.

Children must be exposed to communication and the expression of feelings before they can communicate. Often children from divorced families have gotten into a habit of not verbalizing how they feel. Feeling hurt or abandoned, they may not want to talk or even know how to express their pain. The single parent has the job of turning this around by exposing the child to deeper levels of communication.

PHASE THREE: EXPERIENCE

A child will soon learn to count on those special times of communication as he or she grows into adolescence. When a child knows he has his parent's undivided attention on those special dates, he will learn it is safe to communicate. As one mother put it, "My oldest son and I have been going out to eat a hamburger at the same time every week for years. Now it's the most amazing thing. Those days he unloads his heart at that meal almost as if he just saves it up until our date."

A most difficult task for the single parent will be to listen and to accept what the older child is communicating. The parent may have a strong desire to interrupt the child many times because the parent will feel a need to correct him. It is important, however, to allow the child to express his opinion. The parent should feel free to say that she does not agree with that opinion. It is still important, however, to listen completely and to help the child understand that his right to an opinion is respected.

As a child gets used to being listened to, he will feel much less need to open conversations with statements meant to get his parent's attention. Those opening lines a child uses to signal that he wants to talk will not be necessary. He will come to know that he already has the listening ear and heart of his single parent. His knowledge comes from previous experience.

If there has already been ongoing communication, the child will feel much more freedom when it comes to discussing the difficult situations that arise in his life. The communication will take place because past experience has shown the child that "Mom won't lecture me. She'll help me work this problem out."

PHASE FOUR: ENCOURAGEMENT

It is an encouragement to the child simply to see that despite the single parent's busy schedule, she does not miss their date together. The child also feels encouragement when he is listened to completely during the date. He senses that his opinion is valuable to his parent. Most of all, the child will find tremendous encouragement and nurturing in a home where true feelings can be openly expressed without fear of rejection or ridicule. A home like this may be the only place where the child can be who he really is, without fear of being made to feel foolish. When the child knows he will find empathy from his single parent, true communication is taking place.

IN REVIEW
Principles of Communication
1. Example

To teach the child how to communicate, the single parent should be free to express feelings and listen to the child with complete concentration.

2. Exposure

There should be a time and a place where the young child can be assured he will not be bothering the single parent when he needs to talk.

3. Experience

Quality communication does not happen overnight. It takes time for a child to know that his parent is, indeed, listening.

4. Encouragement

The greatest encouragment to quality communication in the home comes when the child sees he has his parent's attention during quality time, not just whatever time is left over. When the child perceives that he and communication are that important, he will be encouraged to risk expressing his feelings.

HITTING HOME

1. a. How well do I listen?
   b. How often do I take the time to express my feelings?
2. Is there a time that my child and I can communicate on a quality level?
3. Does my child have reason to believe that he can trust me to respect his opinions and feelings?
4. Do I show my child how important I believe our communication is? How?

II

Making It Special

Today, many communities are filled with homes and apartment buildings identical to those around them. Children growing up in these areas may be subconsciously affected by the sameness. Ironically, the unity is only superficial, because each family has its own set of problems and relationships.

In many single-parent homes, the family as a nurturing body has been split. How does a single parent help restore broken spirits within her family?

Often the single-parent home life is so busy that the members of the household may live a strictly regimented existence. The typical single-parent home starts the day with an early breakfast. The children get dressed and are soon after dropped off at school or some form of day care. The single parent then dashes off to work. Eight hours later, she picks up the children. Dinner is prepared and eaten. The dishes are cleaned. The children go from the kitchen, to the television, to the bathtub, and to bed. After this routine, the single parent collapses.

The days of the week are often discerned only by which television program is on: "What day is it today? Why it's the day M*A*S*H is on." Since one parent is doing the job of two, little else varies in the daily routine. As Saturday rolls around, a new activity takes place— cleaning house.

With nothing particularly special or different happening in such a single-parent family, the children may question whether this unit should even be referred to as a family. What makes a family more than a group of people going through a weekly procedure?

A family needs something that provides a special sense of personal and group identification. "What makes the Barnes family any different from the Smith or Jones family?" An event or occasion that breaks the routine of daily life and brings the family members together. Single-parent families can often be so busy that these special events are the very things that are eliminated.

Edith Schaeffer, in her book called *What Is a Family?* refers to these special family times as the things that children place on their imaginary collage of life. As they think of what glues their family together or what the family's purpose is, children often draw on these special events. Another reason for having special times is to help the children see that the family's function is not only for getting chores done. Otherwise the children come to believe that fun takes place only away from the family. In the single-parent home, children who are often feeling negative about their family need more than a clean house. Family members need to be glued together with the joy of sharing something very special.

As various ethnic groups have immigrated to this country, there seem to have been at least two very striking differences between their families and the typical American family. Initially, these ethnic families have often lacked financial resources. Having recently arrived in the United States, they needed some time, often a generation, to assimilate into the mainstream of the American economic system. Yet with all of the financial hardships they were forced to endure, many times their families remained very close and nurturing. The children in these homes often seemed to be extremely dedicated to their families. In fact, the children in these ethnic homes seemed to hold their families in greater respect than did the American children.

A similarity often exists between ethnic families and single-parent families. Both often suffer financial hardships and must work long, hard hours to make ends meet. But this is where the similarities often end. There must be something more than hardship that pulls the family together. Both are struggling economically, and yet one seems to have a tighter bond in their family unit. Though busy, the ethnic homes had (and fortunately many still have) an extra ingredient often lacking in the single-parent home: very special family traditions.

Family traditions hold each family member in the family and make a family special and different from every other one on the block. In the play *The Fiddler on the Roof,* the life of the particular ethnic group—European Jews—was very perilous and trying. They were robbed of almost everything and persecuted. Owning very little materially and constantly battling poverty, they had their emotional stability stretched to the breaking point. The life of these Jews was as precarious as a fiddler playing his instrument while trying to balance on the peak of the roof. As the playwright stated so boldly, there was only one thing that kept the fiddler from falling to his demise and only one thing that kept these oppressed people from giving up. It was their deep, rich traditions. Their traditions were special and made them feel special. Traditions were the glue of their experience as a group. Traditions are just the kind of glue that the single-parent home needs to provide an investment not only in the children, but also in the very family itself.

TWO KINDS OF TRADITIONS

Traditions can be divided into two categories. The first is the seasonal tradition. The second is the constant, ongoing tradition. An ongoing tradition is one which takes place regularly, is not associated with a specific date or event, and takes place simply for the sake of the family.

An ongoing tradition instituted in my home is game night. This takes place one night a week, generally on Thursday night, when the whole family comes together to play a game. One family member may be responsible for choosing the game, while another has the job of selecting and preparing the snack.

Though they may reach an age when they try not to show it, this night can become a very special time for the children. Once game night is instituted, it is important that the single parent does not allow a busy schedule to break this commitment. It is a commitment not to game night, but rather *to the family*.

Many traditions can be incorporated into the routine of a single-parent home to change a dull routine into a more colorful time for the family. Elsewhere I have already mentioned things such as "dating" the children and maintaining daily family devotions. Some families have special traditions about the way the children are put to bed. One family I know of has each person take turns reading from Mark Twain before bedtime—the parent one night; one of the children the next. Traditions like this not only help to make a family fun, but also help family members to get to know each other again. It's a fine way to tune into what others in the family are thinking. Traditions help pull the members of the family back together.

The special events also help to restore laughter to the home. Many single-parent homes have been without joy and laughter for so long that the children have begun to think that only material gifts will bring them joy. Children can be the first to forget how to have fun at home. A Saturday morning tradition of having the children be in charge of making breakfast can be instituted. The sight of their eggs (or the kitchen) may be enough to bring laughter and excitement into the kitchen!

A while back breakfast time had become difficult at Sheridan House. The children seemed grumpy every morning as they appeared for breakfast. One of the house parents decided to remedy this cloud of moodiness with a very special little weekly tradition that worked with startling success.

One Thursday morning the house mother got up early and put food coloring in the scrambled eggs. The twelve boys arrived at the table and stared in dismay at blue scrambled eggs. They complained and stated that we were forcing them to eat sea gull eggs! At first many of the boys refused to eat the eggs. By the end of the breakfast, however, all the children had eaten far more than usual, and there was laughter at the table. Later that day one of our staff was walking down the hall at the school our boys were attending. He soon found that the story about the "sea gull eggs" had made its way to many of the seven hundred students.

On the following Thursday morning the eggs were changed to red. On Wednesday the children would try to guess what color the eggs would be the next day. Thursday mornings the boys would race to the breakfast table with excited anticipation. This little weekly tradition added special excitement to the lives of these children and made them feel special. The boys even became celebrities at school on Thursdays as people asked, "What color were the eggs today?"

Consistently ongoing traditions can help to take the boredom out of a daily routine. Seasonal traditions can also give a child something to look forward to. An example of a very special opportunity for traditions is the Christmas season. In many single-parent homes this particular holiday lasts only a few hours. Once the presents are distributed and then opened, Christmas is over. This type of Christmas celebration tends to leave everyone unfulfilled. This holiday need not be celebrated only on the twenty-fifth of December, however. Christmas can be a whole season of events pointing toward that special day.

A family that I have known for years has a tradition of making their own ornaments. Each year after Thanksgiving the family decides what kind of Christmas tree ornaments they want to make. Then they spend evenings together making them. One year they made dough ornaments, another year they sewed and stuffed ornaments, and still another year they painted balsa wood ornaments. Sometimes they purchase kits, while other years they create their own. The Christmas tree in their house has no store-bought ornaments on it. Better yet, when these children leave home to start their own families, they will take with them the ornaments that they made. This way another generation of family members can carry on a special family tradition.

In my own childhood home a tradition was getting the Christmas tree. Before going to select the tree, my father would always drive us around the neighborhoods to see how people had decorated their homes. It was a long-awaited night when we brought the tree home, put it in the stand, and always begged to begin decorating it immediately. Just as we always asked, we were always told, "No, we can't decorate the tree yet. It has to settle." We knew that would be the reply, but that was the traditional game we played. The night would then end with hot chocolate.

In 1964 my mother died, and my father became a single parent. At this point as a single parent, my father allowed this tradition to fall by the wayside. My father may have thought that we were too old or did not really care. To the contrary, my brother and I both missed it, but neither of us knew how to express it.

Do children ever get too old to appreciate traditions? My wife's family illustrates otherwise. Christmas at the Johnson home is steeped in tradition. Many activities take place during the weeks preceding Christmas, but the most special time for me has always been Christmas Eve. All their lives, no matter where they have lived, my wife, Rosemary, and her three brothers have always celebrated Christmas Eve the same way.

My wife prepared me before we went to her home that first holiday season after our marriage. She told me that the first thing her family did was to attend the Christmas Eve candlelight service at their church. Then

everyone returned home and changed clothing. Each member of the family, parents
included, would change into their flannel
pajamas.

When I heard this for the first time, I was
shocked. "You mean even today, as old as your
brothers are, they are going to celebrate Christmas Eve in flannel pajamas?" I asked.

Rosemary looked at me with bewilderment
and replied, "Of course, it's one of our traditions."

I remember wondering whether they would
really appear around the tree in flannel pajamas now that they were adults with their own
families. I knew, however, that I would be safe.
I had not owned a pair of pajamas in years, let
alone flannel pajamas! There were other traditions connected with Christmas Eve that Rosemary told me about, but the flannel pajamas
kept popping into my mind.

The day finally arrived. Christmas Eve
came, and true to tradition, we were off to the
candlelight service. Following the service, we
walked in the front door of their home, and
everyone disappeared. Moments later, as I
arrived in the living room in my shirt and
slacks, I was stunned to see three generations
of Danes return to the living room in their

flannel pajamas! I felt as if I stuck out like Mr. Scrooge! The birth of Christ was read from the Book of Luke, and this was followed by "'Twas the Night before Christmas." I was amazed as everything went in the exact order that it had for three decades. If anyone would have dared to suggest that a tradition be omitted or changed, the children (who are now adults and parents themselves) might have stoned them!

After a prayer, each person in the room was permitted to open one present. At this point Rosemary and her brothers all became children again and begged to open just one more. This, too, was part of their tradition, and the requests were always denied. My present was handed to me, and since all eyes were upon me, I opened it. As I revealed the contents to all my spectators, there were cheers and howls of laughter. The present I received now made me a full-fledged member of the family! My present was flannel pajamas!

My wife's family had never had much money. They had been missionaries most of their lives. I soon learned, however, that they were very wealthy in family love and commitment. The traditions they had established in their home had become very important. Christmas time was not simply a time of opening presents, but a time of celebrating the birth of Christ and reliving family traditions over thirty years old. One year the youngest boy traveled home all the way from the mission field in Korea. The traditions had made his family that important to him, and he was secure in the knowledge that the Christmas traditions would still be as they had always been.

Many other holidays can be surrounded with traditions. Birthdays are ideal for doing things differently. In my own home special foods always accompany special holidays.

It is not simply the traditions that make a difference to a family. It is the fact that traditions help make each member feel part of a very special unit. Traditions preserve self-worth. If a child of a single-parent home has a low self-image, the very fact that he is a member of a special family that does special things will help to make him feel like a more worthwhile individual.

Family traditions can do much to combat a child's feeling that his family is falling apart. Both the regular, ongoing traditions and seasonal traditions illustrate to the child that his family is still doing special things together. Far too often the only thing members of a single-parent home do together is clean the house. Special events give everyone something to anticipate.

Traditions can be started immediately. Many single parents may read this chapter and say to themselves. "Well, we haven't had any traditions, so I guess it's too late to start." Not so. In my own home we read about or hear about things that other people are doing in their homes. If we feel they will add something to our family life, we adopt them as traditions.

It is often difficult to get children interested in new things, however. When initiating a new tradition, the single parent must be enthusiastic even though the children may not be. After a while the children will catch the enthusiasm and sense the security that comes from knowing the custodial parent is so committed to the family that she will not forget an event that has become a tradition.

IN REVIEW
Principles for Making Families Special
1. Begin and maintain family traditions.
2. It's never too late to start.

HITTING HOME
1. What were the special traditions that you grew up with in your home?
2. What are the fun things that your family does together now?

3. What do you do together in the evenings? During holidays?
4. What do you do together on weekends? During vacations?
5. What do you do as a family that makes you different from other families?
6. What plan do you have to make family time more special?

12

Sex
Education

Probably no area of child training is more
controversial today than the task of teaching
children to properly use the gift of their sexuality. Considerable controversy revolves around
the question "Whose job is it to teach my children about sex?" Many parents today are upset
that the public schools are trying to assume the
task of sex education. In my opinion, these parents are justified in their complaints.

Sex education is much more than a biology
class. One cannot teach a child about sex without incorporating personal values into the lesson. It is not the school's job to impose values
or morals, but simply to instruct its students

objectively in the areas of academic skills. When a school system instructs on the topics of birth control and abortion, it is dealing with personal value systems. On the other hand, it seems that the majority of public schools prefer not to have to teach sex education. The schools feel an urgency to get involved in sex education only because today's family is not teaching its children about sex. Ironically, almost everyone agrees that sex education should be taught within the confines of the family.

For some reason, the parent of today (and even of yesterday) has put off talking to his child about the beauty and function of sex. By the time a parent finally risks talking about sex to the child, it is a long overdue, uncomfortable, and embarrassing lecture. Consequently the necessary lesson may never be taught, or it is conveyed in one quick lecture.

Once at a seminar on training children about their sexuality, I asked the question "How many of you parents were given a lecture about sex only one time in your lives by your parents?" About half of the adults in the audience raised their hands—which surprised me. Presumably the other half that did not raise their hands was indicating that as children they had received more than a one-time lecture about sex. Just then a man in the front row blurted out, "Ask how many of us never received *any* lesson about sex at all from our parents."

I followed this man's advice and posed the question "Of those of you who did not raise your hands, how many of you never had a parent talk to you about sex?" The response was sad. The vast majority of the remaining half raised their hands indicating that of the adults in the auditorium, perhaps 90 percent had received little or no sex education from their parents.

Training a child about sex is more than a biology lesson followed by a list of do's and don'ts. Herein lies the second dilemma. What is a parent to teach? A child should learn about the physical aspects of sex, but also have the opportunity to grow up with an understanding of his or her own gender and sexuality. This is often a most difficult lesson for single parents to teach because they themselves may be struggling with their own sexuality. Sexuality is not confined to the privacy of one's bedroom. A person's sexuality is the way he responds to various situations influenced by his gender, rearing, and cultural background. A woman may appear to be more intuitive in her response to situations in life, whereas a man may appear to respond in a more calculating manner.

In a single-parent home the child does not have the opportunity to see the blend of the two sexes as a man and a woman care for each other and contribute to each other's welfare. When I was a small child, my father knew the importance of illustrating this to me. Before my mother died, my father had a Christmas tradition every year. He would take me Christmas shopping with him one Saturday each December, and we would travel into the city to Macy's Department Store. Together we would go into the lingerie section, and Dad would purchase a negligee for my mother. As a little boy standing there with Dad in the lingerie section, I would be embarrassed to death. I would be in shock at the price he would pay. It never made sense to spend that much money on something like a nightgown. Dad would always explain to me that receiving this from him was important to my mother. Once that annual purchase was made, Dad would take me out for a hamburger.

Back then in my childhood, I always thought that the hamburger was the purpose of the trip. Today I know differently. This annual trip was a part of my training. Dad was showing me that even though we would rather spend the money on a new tool for the shop, it was important for my mother to feel like a woman. My dad was teaching me that women are different from men, and only as I grew up did his lesson come to light. Even when my mother was no longer around, my father was quick to take advantage of any opportunity to talk to us or to illustrate to his boys the emotional differences between men and women.

PHASE ONE: EXAMPLE

While the example the parent sets is important, nothing has more significance or requires more soul searching than the single parent's expression of sexuality. After the separation or divorce the single parent's sexual identity is often in deep confusion. Possibly it was an affair on the part of the spouse that brought about the divorce. Very likely, as with the majority of divorces, some type of sexual incompatibility existed prior to the breakup. That, along with other circumstances, can make the single parent wonder what is wrong with her sexually. The divorce also may make a single parent feel sexually frustrated.

"What am I to do now? I've got the kids and

no prospects for dates. I know that he [ex-husband] is having a wonderful time in his new bachelor pad. It's so difficult to go to bed alone after all these years of marriage. No matter how much we fought, he was still a man to sleep next to at night." This frustrated confession of a single mom could probably be heard from thousands of other women. She had been married and had had some sex life for many years. Then all of a sudden, *nothing*.

The single mother may envy her ex-husband. She may think that because her ex-husband did not have the children, he would not have to stop his sex life. This woman is very wrong about the real purpose of sex, and might subsequently have a difficult time teaching her children. She may also find it very difficult to exist without sexual involvement. The fact that one parent has custody of the child does not keep that parent from becoming sexually involved with his or her dates.

What will help a single parent or an adolescent remain sexually inactive? A proper understanding of the true purpose of sex. God created each of us male or female, and in his wisdom he established our sexuality. Sex is not evil. It is a gift from God to men and women, and is to be handled in a very specific way. God made men and women so that they would be sexually attracted to each other. The many biblical references to marriage and to a husband and a wife becoming one flesh show God's priority for this particular relationship (Genesis 2:24; Matthew 19:5-6; Mark 10:8; Ephesians 5:31). *One flesh* means that a husband and his wife should become so close to each other in every way that they respond to life together as if they were one person.

We develop many relationships in life. The marriage relationship, however, is of such importance that God wants a husband and his wife to have a special experience to enhance their intimacy even further. God wants marriage to be special above all others, and to prove that, he has adorned it with the gift of sexual intercourse. God also enhanced sex by making it the means of conception. Without a doubt, one's sexuality is a gift from God. That is why the single mother quoted earlier in this chapter should have decided to be sexually inactive—not simply because of the children, but because God in his wisdom planned it that way.

The example that the single parent sets must reflect a responsible attitude toward sex. Children in single-parent homes often listen to a father who has reverted back to his adolescent years. The father may be constantly on the lookout for a woman, or he may be trying to overcome his own insecurities by giving his children the impression that a real man brings a different woman home every night. This child grows up thinking that sex is not a sharing experience of love between husband and wife, but rather something to be taken from anyone available.

Some single mothers feel that they have been used sexually and thus portray to the child an ugliness and unholiness about sex. The media also show sex to be little more than a recreational activity. The child must perceive in the single parent an attitude that paints a different picture.

When the single parent dates, she should go out of her way to let the children know what is happening, where she is going, and what time she will be home. The child should be able to see a wholesomeness about his mother's dating relationship and the way she handles her sexuality. Anything that could appear at all questionable should be explained to the child. The single parent has the unique opportunity to teach the child about dating through the example that is given. By the high dating standards that the single parent sets for herself, she is also teaching much about the importance of reserving sexual intercourse for the marriage relationship. Appropriate dress is significant. Spending the night out, no matter how innocent it may be, can create a very poor impression upon young minds which could begin to fantasize in unwholesome ways. The example must be above suspicion.

PHASE TWO: EXPOSURE

Children are exposed to the biological aspects of sex at a very early age. It does not take long for a little boy to discover that he has a certain apparatus that his sister doesn't have. Likewise a little girl is aware that she is made very differently from her brother. One of the first at-home sex education courses is in the area of hygiene. It is important to teach a child how to properly bathe his or her genitals.

Between the ages of three and six could be the most critical time for a child to be taught about sex. At this time the child is open and curious and asks questions. It is natural for a young child to ask about parts of the body and where babies come from because the child is not yet embarrassed about this topic. There will never be another age when the lines of communication concerning sex are so open.

If the very busy single parent is too preoccupied, she can miss the opportunities that a young child makes available with his or her questions. Often the questions are embarrassing to the single parent, and they always seem to come at the wrong time. Still, the single parent must decide what is more important: to continue washing the dishes or to answer questions. The beauty of this age is that one part of the body is no more embarrassing than any other part to a four year old.

Many parents teach a young child fictitious names for parts of the sexual anatomy. These incorrect labels will only have to be corrected later. Other parents simply respond by saying, "I'll tell you later." "Later" never seems to come, and a child can begin to wonder if you just do not talk to adults about that part of the body: *especially since it always seems to make Mom nervous,* the child thinks. It is important to respond to the questions and to give a child the proper labels to work with.

The questions at this age do not stop with anatomy, however. "Where do babies come from?" is a standard question, and the answers are often incredible. Each parent faces that question and makes a decision as to how she will respond to similar questions. Most often the decision is an instant attempt to delay assuming the responsibility of sex education. Anticipating these questions ahead of time helps a single parent formulate an answer.

A single mother of a thirteen-year-old girl once announced that she had not yet told her daughter about sex and did not intend to in the near future. "What my daughter doesn't know can't hurt her," she said. How sad an approach to sex education—and an altogether too common one.

When the question "Where do babies come from?" is asked, the response is usually more of a distraction: "You're too young to know about such things. When you're older we'll discuss it." When the child is older, however, it is very unlikely that he will once again ask the question. This approach simply ignores the obvious opportunity.

A second way of handling the birth question is to make up a story. Responses such as the following are not uncommon:

"The stork brought you."

"The doctor had you in his bag."

"We picked you out at the hospital."

These are just a few of the lies that eventually must be rectified. It is important to give a child a good foundation. As he becomes of school age, he is away from home more often. It is better for him to know the facts from home before the world pollutes the beauty of birth and sex for him.

The questions asked at this age should be accepted as an opportunity. "Mom, where did I come from?" Mom answers, "You came from my tummy." Step by step the child will ask questions that are more and more involved. These should be answered just as any other question would be answered. The single parent must be alert to the questions and grateful for the chance to teach rather than becoming annoyed or embarrassed. The overly busy schedule must be put aside for this important topic.

At this point many single parents will say, "But my child is of the opposite sex! I don't know how to discuss this topic with my child." It is amazing how hard a single mother will struggle to explain football to her son. She may be uncomfortable with the topic of football, but she does not want him to miss out; so she attempts the topic. How much more important is the topic of sex. It is not a single parent's inability that frightens her from telling her son about sex. It is her embarrassment, and yet at this age of innocent questions, the child is not embarrassed at all.

As the questions get more specific, the answers need to be more specific. The following is a sample discussion:

Mother: "You were born because the sperm from your father united with an egg inside my body. That coming together of egg and sperm is what we call conception. Then you grew for nine months in my tummy."

Child: "What is sperm?"

Mother: "A sperm is a little tiny cell, smaller than a grain of salt, that comes from the man to help make babies."

Without a doubt this type of communication seems like an awesome mouthful! And yet questions related to this topic may never be asked again. Your attitude certainly keeps the lines of communication open for future questions and training. Probably at no time does a parent feel totally comfortable discussing sex. There is only one time, however, when a child will feel so free and comfortable about discussing sex, and that is during these early elementary years. This opportunity must be seized.

PHASE THREE: EXPERIENCE

A child actively begins to experience his or her own sexuality as he or she enters puberty. One of the hormones released at this stage of development stimulates the sex glands toward maturity. This can be a moody and emotional time for a child. Once again single parents will need to be extra careful to continue the training even now when the questions are not being asked.

Even though questions may not be verbalized, they are still there. However, if a child's questions have been answered in the past, very likely he will be less embarrassed with these questions at this stage. Often in the mayhem of the single parent's home, the early adolescent does not know how or when to ask the questions. He may put the questions off because now he is embarrassed about these discussions, or maybe he will ask his noncustodial parent when he visits his home. The opportunity probably never surfaces there, either.

The questions, if verbalized at all, are much more guarded. The single parent must learn to listen deeply to what is actually being asked. A single mother confessed to me: "My daughter was ten years old when she asked me, 'How would a girl know if she were pregnant?' I answered her by saying, 'One sure way would be if she missed her period.' My daughter had just begun having her period, and her cycle was still a bit erratic. She had never been involved sexually, and yet she had missed a period. Because of the unthinking way that I answered her question, she was convinced that somehow she was pregnant, and she stayed awake nights worrying about what to do." A question of this kind should not have been taken at face value, but tenderly pursued to find out what the child was really asking. The child should have been aware that babies can not just happen, and that often when a girl is beginning her menstruation cycle, it can be erratic.

Children need to know that the growth of pubic hair and other body changes are all a part of the process of growing up. Young boys do not know how to deal with wet dreams, and their single moms do not know how to tell them that it is a natural phenomenon. Communication may be a strain at this juncture of development, but it is a necessity. If the single parent truly does not know how to approach some of the topics or answer the questions, then a trip to a Christian bookstore would be a wise step. There are numerous books out today that do an excellent job of giving a parent the necessary resource material.

Besides the physical aspect, the early adolescent also needs help in making sense of feelings of attraction to the opposite sex. Here the example of the single parent is so important.

Mother: "Nancy, I know that you are very attracted to this boy that you are seeing. I want you to know that it is natural for the two of you to want to become more and more involved. Sexual urges are not evil—we just need to treat them responsibly. Maybe it's never occurred to you before, but since I'm no longer married, I, too, must face these same urges. A long time ago I decided that sexual intercourse was a relationship that God set apart and reserved for the intimacy of marriage. It is a beautiful sign or expression of the special relationship between a husband and a wife. I decided that I would not defile that, and I hope you will act in the same responsible manner. It's not always easy. Believe me, I know. But it is the way God has planned it."

Knowing that his or her single parent faces the same struggle can make it easier for a young person to discuss his feelings. The discussions should be regular and open even if the adolescent does not initiate the talks. At this age the young people want to know some nitty-gritty facts—how they can know what real love is, what sexual compatibility means, whether girls can have orgasms, and so on. Girls want to know what boys expect from them on dates, what they should be prepared for, and what God expects of them. The questions and fantasies are endless, but the opportunities to ask about them seem rare in the single-parent home.

PHASE FOUR: ENCOURAGEMENT

Pressure to conform to the liberal sexual ethics of today is very strong. The adolescent is in a constant struggle to balance what he or she has been taught with the standards of society. Facing the same pressures can be positive for both parent and child. The single parent is given an opening to ongoing discussions of what God has planned for his children. As difficult as it often is to stay in that plan, be encouraged. If you ask him, God promises to supply the strength and wisdom you need to cope with your child's dating and with your own sexuality. The single parent's openness and willingness to communicate provide additional encouragement and even preventive medicine. A child who feels he must carry his burden alone will make serious mistakes. However, with God, the single parent and young person can feel the special comradeship of sharing in and triumphing over the struggle of premarital sex.

IN REVIEW
Principles of Sex Education
1. Example
   The single parent, who very possibly is also experiencing sexual struggles, must look to God for sexual standards rather than to society.
2. Exposure
   A child should be taught a rudimentary biology of sex at an early age when the opportunity arises through the child's innocent questions.
3. Experience
   As a child enters puberty, he should be taught about the physical and sexual changes that he will be experiencing. He should be helped to understand that his new feelings are part of God's plan, that sex is meant for marriage, and that sexual urges are part of the preparation for finding a mate.

4. Encouragement

The lines of communication must be kept open so that the discussions can be ongoing. This way the young person can feel that he has been understood, rather than lectured to.

HITTING HOME

1. As a single parent, do you have a plan to train your child to grow up to be a sexually responsible adult?
2. How do you handle your own sexual difficulties?
3. Are you alert to opportunities to discuss "the facts of life"?
4. How can you keep the lines of communication open? Can your child ask you questions about sex?
5. Do you have a tendency to get "preachy"? If so, what can you do to reduce preachiness? Does your lecturing help or hinder communication with your child?

13

Sibling Rivalry

"Over the past few years it seems as if my two children can't even sit at the same table and be civil to each other. Most of the time we don't seem like a family at all. It's more like three people who are just barely tolerating each other."

The problem of sibling hostility reflected by this statement is not a difficulty confined only to the single-parent home. It is also found in many other homes. Sibling hostility does, however, seem to be more prevalent in the home where there is only one parent.

The ingredients for helping children become positive family members are many. One is to help children develop healthy self-esteem. Another is making the home a fun place to live. The last ingredient is helping children express themselves before family members and others with a positive attitude.

A child receives his nurturing from his family. The family unit is the very foundation from which children come to know who they are. The family should help them learn to feel good about themselves. This is called self-esteem, which we discussed in chapter 9. When there is a crack in this family "foundation" and separation or divorce takes place, the child's feelings about himself can suffer. It is not only the parents who get divorced but also the child. "Dad, for one reason or another, chose not to live with me," many children think. No matter how hard both parents have worked to dispel from the child the feeling of having been abandoned by Dad, the feeling quite often still lingers. After all, when it is time for bed, Dad is no longer there. He may even be tucking in the children from his new family. As the child ponders on that reality, he can quickly feel that he is a very inadequate individual. When a child (or any person) does not feel good about himself, then it does not take long for him to project those negative feelings to those around him.

Other factors can cause the child of a single-parent home to display a negative attitude. The family is a unifying force for a child. Children learn their first feelings of belonging (esprit de corps) from their membership in a family unit. A small child can experience what it is like for each family member to work as part of a team; for example, while preparing for one team member's birthday or for a special holiday. Family membership teaches children how to commit themselves to a body or group larger than themselves. As the child learns to make a commitment to his family, he can eventually learn to commit himself to a larger body, such as his country.

The family is God's tool to nurture the child and draw the child out of his natural self-centeredness. As a child contributes to the family or makes sacrifices for a family member, he learns to think about the welfare of more people than just himself. Ideally, it is through the strong Christian family that the child learns who God is and how to transfer his ultimate commitment to God.

When a child begins to make this commitment to his family and his family unit or team

is pulled apart by divorce, the child often feels
that he has no other recourse but to revert
back into himself. Other children may have
seen this family camaraderie only at a friend's
house or by watching some of the more whole-
some television shows about families. These
children can also feel the loss. They know what
a family can be like when all members work
together toward a common goal. They also
know that their own personal family does not
function this way. The lack of a family team
attitude or commitment experience only
encourages them to retreat back to their more
immature social habits.

Typically self-centered, little children generally find it very difficult to share or sacrifice
for another person. Part of growing up and
maturing socially is to grow farther and farther away from that self-centeredness. The
retreat back to a self-centered, socially immature attitude takes place when the child feels
that other family members are no longer committed. There can be almost an "every man
for himself" attitude.

One parent through the divorce has already
dissolved his commitment to the family unit.
The child begins to wonder who will go next. As
a defense against further hurt, some children

will follow the lead of the parent who has left and will draw away from making a commitment to the family. Hostility and abusive language toward the remaining family members are signals of this attitude.

Expressing negative attitudes toward the family can also be a learned behavior. Many children from single-parent homes have previously witnessed so much hostility and abuse between their parents that they adopt this same negative behavior as their own. If their adult models have had nothing good to say to each other and mealtimes have been very tense, then the children soon learn that this is the accepted way their family expresses itself.

Often a fear of being loving or kind exists in a hostile family environment. Positive behavior may be seen as weakness and may be met with rejection or worse. This attitude has been transferred from two parents who have a disintegrating relationship. One of the outward manifestations of this is verbal abuse.

It can be viewed as encouraging, however, that a negative attitude toward the family can be a learned behavior. Anything that is learned can be unlearned. The unlearning of negatives and relearning of positives must begin with the single parent.

PHASE ONE: EXAMPLE

Years ago Sheridan House for Youth had a
house parent with a basic philosophy about dealing with children who were very sullen and negative toward others. Often when a new child
would begin his residence at one of the homes
at Sheridan House, he would act as if he were
incapable of saying anything nice to anyone.
The child usually felt so bad about himself that
he tried to make everyone else miserable by
making derogatory comments. When this would
happen, this particular house father would get
the other children together and say, "We need to
help this new child. The only way to defeat the
bad things he says to you is to do what? You tell
me."

Those children had been around this man
long enough to know exactly what they were to
say in response to his question. They always
responded in unison, "Kill him with love and
kindness, Pop."

And this house father named "Pop" would
add, "That's right. No matter what he says to
you, don't fall into his attitude trap. Return his
bad comments with kindness."

The children would try to use the kindness
approach on a child, and some became very

adept at maintaining it for long periods of time. The greatest thing to watch, however, was Pop and his attitude toward each sullen child. This house parent worked hard to keep his particular cottage in beautiful shape, and yet the new sullen child would have nothing but negative comments to make about his new home. No matter what the child said or how badly the comments might have hurt Pop, he never fell into the trap. He never snapped back at the child. Pop would make nothing but positive, encouraging comments. He would not accept behavior that was unacceptable, but he still made it obvious that he thought each child had good qualities.

While a sullen child would try to maintain his negative attitude, the example of Pop would eventually win him over. This kind of example can also work in the single-parent home. Children can be taught how to take the risk and say something positive about the family or a sibling.

Like Pop, the single parent can set this kind of example in her home. When no one else has anything positive to say, it may be because it has been a long time since anyone has heard anybody else make a positive comment.

Mealtime is ideal for initiating positives. The

single parent has an opportunity to say nice things to each child while all are there to hear them.

> *Parent:* "I really appreciated your help with the table tonight, Bobby."
> *Child:* "All I did was put the napkins out."
> *Parent:* "That little bit helps me get more accomplished. Thank you for taking the time to help me."

If the single parent takes the time to search for any opportunity to say positive things (and sometimes it will take quite a bit of searching), it will be the start of the lesson. The child will begin to be drawn back into the family and to search for more ways to hear positive comments about himself.

Our society seems to encourage negative statements. People search for what is wrong with things rather than what is right about them. The media are not concerned about reporting the good things that happen in our world. It is the shocking and the sensational that sell newspapers. However, when a person comes along with a positive attitude, people seem to feel better just being around him. The single parent must become that person.

As with everyone else, the single parent

could focus on all the bad things that have been, and still are, happening. That kind of attitude would not improve the situation. If for no other reason than the growth of the children, the single parent must decide to focus on the positive things in life. Eventually the children will catch on. The fact that today there is a roof to sleep under and food on the table is more of a positive than many of us realize. A large portion of the world is not so fortunate.

More importantly, focusing on the positive can also help the child realize that there is still a family living in the house—not just a few boarders living together. Despite the divorce and the painful disruption it has caused, the single parent and the children do not need to act as if they are dealing with it all alone. They have each other and the Lord. If the single parent can set an example by showing a grateful attitude, it will encourage the children to reinvest in their family.

PHASE TWO: EXPOSURE

Sometimes children would like to make positive statements, but they just cannot quite get them out. It may have been a long time since the child has said anything of a positive nature to his sister. If he did she might laugh, or so he thinks. In situations like these the single parent can orchestrate the dialogue by helping the child with the words.

Parent: "Billy, your sister made your favorite dessert tonight. Isn't it delicious?"

This is an example of helping Billy by putting the words in his mouth. He is probably out of practice and needs this kind of help. Initially, a positive response may be almost more than he can handle. He may start out with: "She made this? I'm poisoned!" In cases like this, it is always important to stay calm and respond with love and humor.

Parent: "I agree. It even tastes so bad that I am going to have another piece. Do you want some more poison cake?"

Eventually, exposure to positive comments and opportunities to speak will encourage the child to take a risk.

Billy: "Yes, this is a great cake!"

The point here, as sad as it sounds, is that many children reach such a low point in their own self-esteem that they need to be handed a new script. When the single parent virtually put the words into Billy's mouth, it helped him get started with positives.

PHASE THREE: EXPERIENCE

The scribes tried to trap Christ with the question of which commandment was the greatest. He responded by saying that there were two important commands, and the second one is to love your neighbor as yourself (Matthew 22:39). The act of learning to love the people around you does not come naturally. It takes training and faith in Christ. The training aspect must begin in the home.

As the child in the single-parent home reverts back to that self-centered attitude that he had grown out of years ago, the parent must help him experience relearning how to love the members of the family. Love should be seen by the child as a verb, or an action. To experience loving the other members of the family, he should be helped to do deeds of love.

Billy can be given the opportunity to do things for his sister. Her bicycle may need to be worked on (or something else that belongs to her may be in disrepair). Billy might also enjoy (though he will probably try to hide his enthusiasm) cooking for his sister. At the completion of any of these deeds of love, his sister can be given a chance to express her gratitude.

> *Parent:* "What did you think about Billy doing all of that work for you?"
> *Debby:* "Thank you, Billy, I really appreciate what you did."
> *Parent:* "How did it make you think your brother feels about you?"
> *Debby:* "I don't know."
> *Parent:* "It made me feel that he did it because he loves you."

These conversations should take place when all parties are present, in order for there to be maximum benefit.

Birthdays and holidays are also special times to help children do things for each other. One child can help shop, decorate, and bake a cake for the other child's birthday. These special occasions are ready-made opportunities to teach siblings to express their love for each other.

There is an important thing to remember. The single parent should not stop the training experience with just the good deeds. A response about his feelings should be elicited from the child.

Parent: "How did it make you feel when you saw that Billy had done this for you?"
Debby: "It made me feel good."
Parent: "Why do you think Billy did it for you?"
Debby: "I guess because he loves me."
Parent: "Is that right, Billy? Did you do this for Debby because you love your sister?"
Billy: "Yes."

It is very important to take advantage of every opportunity to elicit positive conversation between siblings, even if the single parent has to be the moderator. As these experiences add up, the children will begin to feel more comfortable about risking unsolicited positive comments.

PHASE FOUR: ENCOURAGEMENT
A child in a single-parent home who consciously or subconsciously has made a decision to distance himself from the family (for any or all of the reasons previously listed) will find it very difficult to turn around and once again become a positive loving family member.

The break-up of the family or the child's fantasies about what his family should be like may have caused him great enough pain not to want to risk the pain again. Isolation and self-centeredness may be his defense. If he is negative enough or critical enough of other family members, they will not try to pull him back into the family. The child can just hang out in his room with the door closed. Even at the dinner table when the family is together, he will try to keep the door to his family involvement closed.

This kind of defense can never be overcome without great difficulty and patient encouragement. Of all the four stages where this particular training is concerned, encouragement is the most important ingredient. Anytime the child sticks his head through that imaginary closed door and risks involvement or risks saying something positive, he should be encouraged for it.

Parent: "I really appreciated the way you complimented your sister on the meal. It made her feel good and it also made me feel good to hear you encourage her. Thank you for saying it."

Billy may feel very awkward saying something positive to his sister, and she may not respond in such a way that shows him how much it meant. It is the single parent who can tell Billy how much those positive comments are appreciated. Quite often the lack of response from the child to the single parent's attempt at making an encouraging statement makes the single parent herself feel that she is wasting her time. Years ago I was shown how wrong that is.

I knew it was important to encourage the children at Sheridan House. When they did something positive, I would encourage them verbally and then again in writing. At that time I carried around a small yellow pad. When I saw a child make a positive contribution, I would say something to the child like, "That was a nice thing to say, Johnny." Then to further encourage Johnny, I would write a little note on the yellow pad, fold it, and put it on his bed. The note might have said:

Last night at the dinner table I was impressed by the way you complimented Greg on the grade he got on his spelling test. Thank you for being an encourager.

Saying things like that will help our family here at Sheridan House. Thank you.

When Johnny got home from school, he would find my note encouraging him to continue making those positive comments. Some children so rarely hear positive things about themselves that I felt it would be even more valuable for them to see it also in writing.

Never once during the several months of writing these notes did I ever hear anything positive about them from the children. I personally received no encouragement for my positive contribution of the notes. Even though there was a change in the attitudes of many of the boys during this time period, I began to feel that the notes meant nothing. A few months later I discontinued writing the encouraging words and instead just verbalized my encouragements.

Not long after that, a boy was preparing to go home from Sheridan House. I was in his room talking with him and helping him pack. He was almost finished putting all of his clothes in his suitcase when he reached into the back of a drawer and pulled out a neatly stacked pile of those little yellow notes. The child had saved every one of those notes as if they were medals proving that he was a good person, and he was taking them home. I must say I had to fight back tears.

Most children are starved for encouragement, and words or notes are proof to them that they are indeed worthy of receiving encouragement. This boy was not quite confident enough to say thank-you for the yellow notes. Unfortunately, I was not quite secure enough to continue doing something I knew was right to do. At that time I was not adult enough to continue making those positive contributions to the "family" without receiving encouragement myself.

Far too many children hear more negatives about themselves than they do any positives. Under these circumstances it doesn't take long until their own positive contributions to the family become less and less frequent. Thus the parent seems to have less to encourage the child about. It becomes a descending spiral, which is up to the parent to break. A child in a single-parent home is usually desperate to be encouraged for anything. As he hears more and more positive encouragement from his single parent, he will eventually risk becoming more positively involved with his family.

It takes a long period of encouragement before the child will feel it is worth the risk of saying nice things to other members of the family. Slowly the child should feel that it is worth the risk of opening himself up and becoming a positive, contributing team member of the family.

It has been said that a positive attitude and positive comments are contagious. I believe that this is true, just as I believe that a negative attitude can also be catching. In order to help siblings get along with each other and with the family in general, the single parent must set the tone.

IN REVIEW

Principles for Reducing Sibling Rivalry

1. Example

The single parent must adopt a positive attitude about each family member, and must be alert to opportunities to say positive things.

2. Exposure

The single parent can help children develop a positive attitude toward siblings by helping them say positive things to their brothers and sisters.

3. Experience

Children can be given the opportunity to do things for each other, and then they can be helped to express their gratitude and love for each other.

4. Encouragement

The single parent should become a great encourager. Anytime a child risks making a positive statement, he should receive an abundant amount of praise and encouragement.

HITTING HOME

As a single parent, do you set the tone in your home for the children to act in a loving way toward each other?

1. If the children acted like you, would they be positive or negative in their verbal responses to each other?

2. Keep a small pad near by you all day Sunday. Draw a line down the middle and write *P* for positive and *N* for negative on the other side. Keep score and see whether you make more negative or positive comments to the children.

3. What kinds of comments could you use to help the children say positive things to each other?

4. What kinds of things could your children do for each other?

5. What is your plan to help you become an encourager?

14

Discipline

The greatest lessons I learned about discipline
came in 1974 when I arrived at Sheridan
House. At that time it consisted of only one
home for boys. These boys—a dozen twelve to
sixteen year olds—came predominantly from
single-parent homes. I was just a few years out
of school when I was hired as the new director.
My plans for this program included putting my
degrees on the wall, arranging all my professional books, and counseling the boys!

God had different plans for me. Not long
after I had gotten my books in order, the house
parents of the boys' home walked into my
office to announce that they were resigning.
That was only the first shock. The second one
came when I realized that there was no one

around to replace them during the forty-five day interim period before new house parents would arrive. That is, there was no one but Bob Barnes.

After recovering from the shock, I moved into the boys' home with the feeble confidence that I, after all, had been to school and had read the books. All I felt I needed to do was open the lines of communication with the boys and be very encouraging to them. I now know how badly I needed that forty-five day experience!

My second night in the home, the boys were watching television, and I announced, "At nine o'clock I want the TV turned off, and all of you to go to bed." After making that proclamation, I walked out of the living room and into another room to read. I was confident they had understood my wishes. At 9:10 I heard a disconcerting noise coming from the living room. I decided, or probably I should say *hoped,* that the boys had gone to bed, but had left the television on. As I walked into the living room to turn it off, I was met by several pairs of very anxious eyes. Some of the boys had gone to bed as they were told, but several were still up. Their look told me that I could not assume they had misunderstood me. They knew what my request was, they just were not sure whether I had been serious about it or not. I was somewhat shocked and helped them off to bed.

Twenty minutes later, the boys were under their covers and the house was quiet. I returned to my reading somewhat perplexed about the fact that I seemed to have had such little control in that particular situation, but I was glad that it was over. As I pondered this, a familiar noise once again came to my ears. The television was once again on, and it was just loud enough for the whole house to know that it was on.

As I walked into the living room hoping to find that this set had a malfunction in it and had turned on by itself, my hopes were dashed. There in front of the television set sat a very sullen, little thirteen year old named Al. He was one of the boys who had been at Sheridan House the longest.

My first act was to turn off the television. At this point Al blurted out, "Hey, what are you doing? I was watching that." This very moment would prove to be one of the most significant times for me in this house. I asked Al if he had heard me say that no one was to get out of bed, knowing full well that he had heard. His reply was that he wanted to watch something on television. As he said that, Al looked me right in the eyes as if he were really saying, "Who's in charge here, you or me?" His obvious rebellion was, in reality, a test of my commitment to these boys and their home.

"Al, you need to come with me," I said, not quite sure what I was going to do. Nothing in my training had prepared me for this kind of involvement. I knew one thing. The decision that I was to make at that moment would tell all the boys, not just Al, whether or not rebellion would be an acceptable form of behavior.

Al and I walked into my office and looked at each other. I announced that he had willfully disobeyed my command, and he admitted to that. I then announced that the consequence for rebellion was a spanking. He tried to look shocked and even made an attempt at an argument. I told him that he had chosen to accept whatever the punishment would be, when he had chosen to rebel against the authority of that home. I asked this child to bend over my chair; then for the first time in my life, I used a small paddle and gave a boy a spanking. Following this spanking and the tears came a time of sitting together on the couch and talking. Now that the boundaries were set for appropriate and acceptable behavior, we were able to begin our relationship.

Al went on to bed, and I sat up most of the night somewhat in shock. Most of my training had taught me that corporal punishment was outdated. I had no books to turn to except my Bible. I was searching for reassurance, and two verses in Proverbs helped me immensely. Proverbs 22:15 (KJV) instructed that spanking is the correct form of discipline to use when a child is rebellious. It also stated that I was to use an instrument other than my hand. I was encouraged to find that I had dealt with rebellion according to God's instructions.

Now years later, I have come to realize that a wooden spoon or a paddle is an instrument that is removed from my body. My hand is too convenient. I never want to slap a child instantaneously out of anger, rather than for the purpose of correction.

Spanking is meant to meet the child's needs when he is rebellious. It is not a time for a single parent to vent anger. Far too many parents spank children for the wrong reasons. A child should be spanked when he needs it, not when the parent needs to do it.

God has also supplied a specific location for

the spanking to be applied—on the child's but-
tocks. When Al was spanked that night, he
cried because it hurt and also out of emotional
relief from the end of the power struggle.

The spanking came immediately after the
rebellion. I could have said, "It's too late to deal
with this now, Al. Go to bed and I'll administer
the punishment in the morning." I wanted to do
that, but it would have sent Al off to bed even
more frustrated and anxious. The spanking
needed to be handled in an orderly, controlled
manner, and as it says in Proverbs 13:24, he
needed to be admonished promptly. Al had very
little time to worry or become anxious about his
punishment.

Rebellion had sent a wave of insecurity and
fear through the home. The boys all wondered
if this new man Mr. Barnes was going to be
able to bring stability back into their family setting. The only way they could find out was to
test it. At a later point, I found a verse that
reassured me of the need to deal with rebellion. First Samuel 15:23 refers to rebellion as
one of the most base of sins when it says, "For
rebellion is as bad as the sin of witchcraft, and
stubbornness is as bad as worshiping idols."
After reading this, I was further convinced that
rebellion must be dealt with. Because God had

put these children in my care, I had to be the one who needed to confront them.

If I needed further encouragement about the ordeal of that night, it came the following morning. I awakened the boys at the usual time, but was shocked to see them get out of bed the first time I called. The previous morning I had to call them several times. This morning they got up, got dressed, came to breakfast, and were in the best mood I had ever seen them. It was as if the insecurity and apprehensions were over. There were now boundaries in their lives, and they could have a wonderful time playing within bounds.

To further amaze me, Al was my big helper that morning. Al and I had a wonderful time together. The boys and I had learned a tremendous lesson. *Children are much more secure in an environment where they feel protected by structure.* Not a stifling structure set up purely for the convenience of the single parent, but rather a structure set up for the growth and protection of the child.

To make these boys more secure in their home, I realized that the next step was to present to them the boundaries for that home. By knowing the rules, they were free to have fun within bounds. Knowing the rules meant that there was no need to wonder or to worry about doing something wrong. They would already know that they were free to choose to do right or wrong and that by breaking a rule, they themselves would be asking for the punishment. This story is not to suggest that a rebellious spirit can necessarily be corrected by one spanking. The authority of the parent might be challenged regularly. Still, I needed a clear, concise plan for this home.

THE PLAN

Many single parents feel the need to discipline their children in one way or another, but things may have gotten so out of hand that they no longer know what to do. A power struggle between parent and child often exists in many single-parent homes. A single parent might establish a plan for structure without putting much thought into it. As soon as a child tests the parent's authority, the parent changes her mind or backs down.

The first step the single parent must do to create structure in the home is to decide which issues need to be dealt with and how they will be dealt with for the child's maximum benefit. The parent must decide the rules that should be established for the child to obey. The rules should be clear and concise so that the child understands them without a doubt. Once a rule is decided upon (a rule that is so important that it is worth pursuing), then the single parent must decide what the consequences will be for violating the rule. A reward can also be established for obeying the rule with a good attitude.

A decision about consequences can be approached in several ways. A single parent can utilize input from a friend or a prayer partner. The two of them can meet and discuss the rules. The more objective point of view of the friend can help the single parent analyze the importance of the rules. Another possibility could be for a single parent to enumerate the rules and then to ask the child to sit and discuss his thoughts about appropriate consequences. Oftentimes some children, in their attempt to get involved in the decision-making process, even suggest punishments that are too harsh. Other single parents feel that neither of these two options is appropriate and that the parent should establish the rules by herself.

Consequences are the most effective when they are logical and fit the violations. Many times I have had single parents tell me that they have a very difficult time getting their children to bed on time at night, and then in the morning they find it even more difficult getting the children out of bed. This situation can serve as a good example of how to institute logical consequences.

My first response to this problem is "Whose responsibility is it for your child to get out of bed in the morning?"

"Well, it's his responsibility to get up," the single parent generally replies. "I just call him."

I then ask, "Oh, you just call him once, and then make it his responsibility to get up."

"No," the parent says, "I keep going back into his room and calling until I get loud enough for him to know that I mean business."

In this situation the child has not yet been given the responsibility of getting out of bed. The single parent has taken the responsibility of going back into the room enough times until it is so uncomfortable for the child that due to the yelling he finally gets out of bed. He has no responsibility in the matter; his single parent accepts it all.

What is the logical consequence for this situation? What is the penalty that this particular single parent has instituted for the child's not getting out of bed on his own? No one really knows because the single parent does not give the child that option. She simply yells until both parent and child are in a bad mood, and the child finally gets out of bed to avoid the noise. If getting up in the morning is a problem between parent and child, then a plan that will remove the parent from the scene as much as possible needs to be established.

The first step is to place the responsibility where it belongs—with the child. The single parent must establish the rule and then back away, resisting the temptation to nag. The child must face the rule rather than the single parent.

The next step is to determine the consequence. A logical consequence for a child who does not seem able to get out of bed in the morning would be for him to go to bed earlier that night. If the child normally goes to bed at nine o'clock each night and finds it difficult to get up the following morning, the logical assumption is that he needs more sleep. The parent may know that this is not the reason for the early morning laziness, but going to bed early for a child is a most profound punishment. For some reason which is unparalleled in adult life, children detest going to bed early!

COMMUNICATION
In order to convey properly that the responsibility is in the child's hands, the parent must

thoroughly explain the new rules and consequences. Here is a sample conversation.

Parent: "You and I have been having a difficult time with each other in the mornings, and so I've decided to try a plan that will help us. This plan will help me not get upset and yell at you when you stay in bed after I've called you. I'm going to place all the responsibility for getting out of bed on your shoulders, because I think you're old enough now.

"Here's how the plan works. You'll continue to go to bed at 9:00 P.M., and the following morning I'll be calling you only one time. After I call you to get up in the morning, I won't come back into your room until after breakfast. If you're not dressed and down to breakfast by 7:00 A.M., I'll assume that you didn't get enough sleep the night before. That night you'll go to bed at 8:00 P.M.

"If, however, you're able to get out of bed after I've called you just one time, then you'll once again be able to stay up until 9:00 P.M. If you can accept the responsibility to get up after one calling and be at breakfast by 7:00 A.M. every day for a week, then we'll discuss letting you stay up until

9:30 P.M. the following week. This will last as long as you're responsible enough to continue getting up on time.

"Remember that the responsibility is on your shoulders. I won't be calling you eight times. Do you feel that you understand this new plan?"

Child: "Yes."

Parent: "Good. Who decides when you go to bed?"

Child: "You do."

Parent: "No, I don't. You decide whether you go to bed at 8:00, 9:00, or 9:30, by how well you accept the responsibility of getting up in the mornings."

Once the message has been communicated, the single parent must resist the temptation to go back and once again assume the responsibility of calling the child more than once in the morning. It must become the child's responsibility.

RESPONSIBILITY

The burden of responsibility must lie with the child, but the single parent must also be consistent in the way the consequences are handled. If the child breaks a rule—and he will, simply to see how it will be handled—the single parent must follow through with the consequences. The child will learn only through consistency that when he breaks the rules, the consequences will always be applied.

Eventually the child will begin to realize he is punishing himself and pitting himself against the rules, not his parent. He will see that when he chooses to violate the rule, he chooses to accept the consequences. The child is responsible for his behavior under these circumstances. He is also responsible for accepting the punishment that he asked for in breaking the rule. Only consistency will drive this message of responsibility home.

When a single parent, with her busy schedule, chooses to apply the punishment sometimes and other times not, the child learns a different lesson. The child sees that it is not really the rules that he is dealing with, but rather the whims of his parent. If he argues long enough, she may once again change her mind. No personal responsibility is being taught under these circumstances. Instead, the child learns how to make his already overburdened single parent miserable enough to give in to his demands.

This kind of inconsistency is neither fair to the child, nor conducive to peace within the home. Children are much more secure when they know what the rules are and that they will be enforced. When the parent is always willing to take the time consistently to enforce the rules, the child will learn to accept the responsibility for his behavior.

CONSEQUENCES

The choice of consequences must be appropriate to the offense and age of the child. A young child should not be punished for childish actions. Spankings are appropriate for rebellion, but certainly not for spilling milk or wetting the bed. Spanking should be reserved for times when a child directly defies the authority of the single parent.

Once the punishment is over, it is very important for the child to know that he has been forgiven. The incident should not be brought up again, because he has paid the price for the infraction. It is also important for the child to know that he was punished *because* he is loved. A parent must be careful to verbalize that she loves the child enough to help him become a better person. The child must come to understand that it is his behavior that is unacceptable, not him as a person.

The final and perhaps most important part of the consequence takes place after the child has received punishment. The parent must then spend time with the child, reaffirming her love for the child. Physical contact such as a hug is very important to help the child to know that he is still loved and that his behavior has been forgiven. Frequently, the punishment is administered, but this reassurance is overlooked. This encouragement time is just as important for the training of the child as is the punishment. Children must know why they have been punished and that by their behavior they are actually demanding their single parent administer these consequences.

The parent did not choose to punish the child; the *child* chose to be punished. As children grow in their acceptance of responsibility, they should be helped to understand this concept. In the atmosphere of loving and talking, this can be taught to a child.

IMPORTANT WORDS ABOUT PUNISHMENT

Child abuse is rampant in today's world. That is one reason why it is important for the single parent to establish a discipline plan and stick with it. Without a plan, the busy, frustrated single parent can easily make decisions about punishment that are far too severe. Decisions of this kind are made out of anger, rather than out of a loving desire to train the child. To tell a child that he is grounded for three months is a consequence not only too severe, but also impossible for the single parent to maintain consistently.

Single parents are often very frustrated when it comes to the parental job of appropriate consequences and awards. That is why they must take time to establish a plan. With a plan the child can be helped to see that every time he performs a certain unacceptable behavior, he will be punished. Eventually, it will occur to him that he is, in fact, punishing himself.

Another indispensable ingredient in discipline is love. A single parent who does not take the time to balance the scales with an abundance of love and acceptance does not have the right to discipline that child. Children must know that they are loved. They must know that it is only their negative behavior that is not loved. Discipline without overt love is a form of emotional child abuse.

IN REVIEW
Principles of Discipline
1. Consistent discipline balanced with an abundance of love can help produce happy, stable, mature, and responsible children.
2. The single parent must deal with unacceptable behavior and rebellion.
3. The parent must first establish a plan that includes consequences appropriate to the undesired behavior of the child.
4. The plan must next be clearly communicated to the child. The parent must be sure that the child understands the plan.
5. The parent must adhere to the plan consistently.
6. Consistency in the home will help the child to know he is the one who is punishing himself.
7. The child must sense that he is cherished, but that his bad behavior is not.

HITTING HOME
1. Example
   a. What type of disciplinarian are you? Consistent/Inconsistent? Peaceful/Angry?
   b. Does love or anger characterize your attempts at disciplining your child(ren)?

    c. Analyze your method of discipline. Does it include love, consistency, and appropriate consequences for undesirable behavior?

2. Exposure
    a. Does your family understand your method of discipline?
    b. Have you discussed discipline with your family? What changes in your discipline style would make yours a happier, more responsible family?

3. Experience
    a. Does your family know that
        (1) you cherish each member? Are you sure?
        (2) you expect them to be *responsible* for their behavior?
        (3) you are consistent in your discipline?
    b. Does your family feel that consequences for inappropriate behavior consistently fit the situation or are consequences more tailored to your moods?

4. Encouragement
    a. Do you encourage your family members when they follow "house rules"? How?

15

Chores and Responsibilities

"It's so much easier to do it myself. Robbie is supposed to do the dishes each night, but the kitchen is a bigger mess when he finishes than it was before he started cleaning it. If teaching him how to do these chores is supposed to save me time, then we've failed. I'd rather avoid the hassle and do it myself."

The above quotation raises the question "What is the true purpose of chores in the home?" The single parent needs an answer to this question before committing herself to the establishment of chores for her children.

In past generations chores around the house were taken for granted. Few time-saving appliances were available. Everyone had to do his part, and the children started at a very young age—gathering the eggs, feeding the animals, making the beds, and so on. Every family member needed to share the load.

Today the single-parent home is in a similar situation. The single parent never seems to have enough time or hands to do the things that need to be done. For the home with one parent, assigning chores is one way to help.

One single parent told me, "In my life as a single parent, time to do the things I need to do is my most precious resource. I can do the chores faster than I can teach them to my child." Another single parent said that it was easier for her to pay somebody else to cut the lawn rather than to have her fourteen year old do it. Both confessions show one thing. We have lost an understanding of the real purpose of family chores.

Giving a child a chore is a valuable lesson for the child and an opportunity to promote family unity. A single parent may quickly say, "I don't care to have my child cut the grass in order to teach him a lesson. Hopefully, he is not going to grow up to be a lawn man." The lesson taught to the child is one on how to accept responsibility.

Most people are aware of 4-H clubs, a youth organization in the farming community that teaches *responsibility* as one of its main goals. Children in 4-H clubs learn many things about agriculture. One of the most important activities of the club is to give a child a baby animal, such as a calf or a pig, to raise. When a child takes on the project, he accepts the long-term responsibility of caring for all the needs of that animal as it grows up. It is an awesome and laborious job, but the child can learn a great lesson. He may not grow up to be a farmer and so he may or may not need to know about animal husbandry. However, what he learns will hold him in good stead for life—accepting various responsibilities as they come his way. Likewise chores in the home should also be aimed at making a child an expert in assuming life's responsibilities, not at making him an expert bed maker.

Establishing routine chores in the home will help the family for today and prepare the child for the world he encounters tomorrow.

At Sheridan House every child in each of the homes has a specific weekly chore to accomplish. We call these chores "responsibilities."

Every Monday they are posted on a bulletin board so each child can see what he is responsible for during that week.

A child may be in charge of vacuuming the house, but we care more about his personal development in this area than we do about the carpets. The key to teaching him to become a responsible person is our attitude. We do not treat him like a machine. The house parent does not follow around behind the child, constantly reminding him to vacuum the carpets. If we did that, then we would be accepting the responsibility for vacuuming. The child would simply be the robot we were using to accomplish the job. Instead, it becomes the child's responsibility to remember to do the job. It is never mentioned to him again once he has been made aware of it on Monday, but he knows that the job must be completed by Friday at 5:00 P.M. If he has not fulfilled his responsibility by this specific time, a consequence is instituted. The boy receives no allowance and his weekend is affected. His house parent does not yell or scream at him for not vacuuming. The consequences are enough. The purpose of this exercise is not to have clean carpets, although that is a nice side benefit. The purpose is to teach children to be responsible.

Responsibility means that a child will take

the initiative to see that a task is accomplished. He must do this without the prompting and nagging of his parent. It also means he will learn to do a job correctly and without being told.

There is a second purpose for teaching responsibility in the home. Often a child reaches adolescence and feels that he does not really belong in the family. Because he has perhaps not been required to take on any particular family responsibility, he is not sure he is part of the family team. Doing chores can help a child feel that he is investing in his family.

Teaching a child to be responsible for specific chores can give the single parent additional opportunities to praise the child. Children basically want to be working members of the family team. It is just not in their nature to begin the investment on their own. Single parents must take the initiative to teach their children how to accept responsibilities within the family. Ultimately, as a child learns to accept responsibility around the home, the time that is saved by his efforts will be an added bonus to the parent and to the entire family. While this is not the purpose for teaching a child to be responsible, it is certainly a rewarding by-product, once the lesson has been learned.

PHASE ONE: EXAMPLE

Research on divorce suggests that it generally takes about two years for the single parent to get her life back in order. It is obvious that before a single parent can teach her child how to be a responsible individual, she must have made strides in this area herself. A child spends much of his time balancing the conflicting feelings he has about acting mature. He wants to act like an adult, and yet he also enjoys the childish privileges of shunning responsibility. He would like to make the right decisions and follow through on the promises that he makes, just as a mature adult would do. Yet, it is easier for him to "forget" or at least seem to forget those promises. The single parent can be a bold example of the importance of being a responsible person.

When I was a child and my father was raising me and my brother, I remember an incident that took place concerning the example he had set for his children. One of my father's responsibilities was to take out the garbage on Tuesday and Friday mornings. The night before each of those mornings he would sail through each of the rooms in the house right after dinner and collect the trash. As he went, he would always seem to be in a good mood. Dad would do this the same time each week and never miss putting it out by the curb that following morning. Pulling into the driveway after work Tuesday night, he would stop the car, pick up the cans, put them where they belonged, and then put the car away. It was like clockwork. We could count on seeing this process take place as we could count on the sun coming up. That is, of course, until he passed this duty on to me.

The day finally came when I was given the responsibility of the Tuesday and Friday trash brigade. I struggled, complained, and agonized over this fifteen-minute job. It was a job I had somehow turned into drudgery. One day when my father and I were discussing this particular responsibility, I said, "It's easy for you to say, Dad. You used to like doing it."

My father laughed and replied, "I disliked that job as much as you, but it had to be done; so I decided to do it to the very best of my ability, without missing a day." I was shocked. I guess I had not thought about it very much and just assumed by the meticulous way that he did it that he actually enjoyed emptying trash cans and carrying them back from the street. I did not realize that he was accepting this dreaded task as a challenge. More importantly, however, was that he was taking advantage of an opportunity to set an example for the young eyes that were watching him.

Single parents should look for opportunities to set the example that they wish to see lived out in their children. If keeping a bedroom clean is one of the responsibilities that the child is to learn, the parent's bedroom should be an example for him to follow. Children can be shown the division of chores among the family members, and then they can observe the way their single parent accepts the responsibility for her own particular jobs.

Regardless of what I was told as a child about accepting responsibility, the greatest impact on my life was the way my single parent accomplished the household tasks to which he had committed himself. Rain or shine the garbage chore got done. Not necessarily because it had to be done at that moment, but because he was teaching his children the importance of accepting responsibility.

PHASE TWO: EXPOSURE
Children in the single-parent home often think that the tedious household chores rob them of time with their parent. For this reason, as well

as for the excitement of acting older, children are usually anxious to spend time with their parent learning how to take on a new responsibility. The exposure stage means that the single parent and the child spend time doing a chore together and thus create another opportunity to be with each other.

A child can begin chores at a very early age. A four year old can be given the project of feeding the cat. With close daily supervision from the single parent, the child can be taught more than simply how to empty a can of food into a bowl. The cat can be fed at the same time each day, possibly in conjunction with a regular event like breakfast or dinner. Just before the family eats breakfast and dinner, parent and child can develop the habit of feeding the cat.

Children work very well in a structured setting or routine. It will not take long until the young child is able to remind the adult, "We can't eat yet, Mommy. We forgot to feed Fluffy." When this begins to happen, the child changes the feeding of Fluffy from a chore to a responsibility. Exposure to the feeding of the cat means that the parent is still taking the responsibility to see that the chore gets done, even if the child actually does it. At this point it is still just a chore as far as the child is concerned. The feeding of Fluffy becomes a responsibility for the child when he *remembers* to do the chore and actually feeds the cat without being told or supervised.

The main purpose of any chore is not to relieve the single parent of a job, though that should happen later on. The primary purpose is to teach the child how to accept responsibilities. The exposure stage may be time-consuming, but it can also be made into a fun activity for parent and child. Whether the chore is making a bed, cutting the lawn, emptying the dishwasher, or vacuuming a room, the child is given an opportunity to do something with his parent. Without a doubt, the attitude of the parent toward the chore being done greatly influences the child's own attitude.

PHASE THREE: EXPERIENCE
This is the point at which the child accepts the chore as his personal responsibility. The declaration of this responsibility can be handled in many ways, but it must be explained thoroughly.

Parent: "We've been feeding Fluffy together for a long time now, and I believe that you've learned how to do a good job at this chore.

It's now time for you to be responsible for this. I won't be reminding you twice a day to feed the cat. You must remember."

Jimmy: "I can't remember, Mom."

Parent: "I know you can. When do you feed Fluffy each day?"

Jimmy: "I feed Fluffy just before breakfast and just before dinner."

Parent: "That's right, Jimmy. So when you sit down at breakfast and dinner and remember that you forgot to feed Fluffy, you'll have to excuse yourself and go do it. But remember, I won't be reminding you to do it each day. It is *your* responsibility. Fluffy will be depending on you."

Jimmy: "I can do it, Mom."

Jimmy will be excited about this new thing called "responsibility" for about two days. At that point of the experience phase comes the real test for the single parent. Jimmy will forget to feed Fluffy. In order for the parent to show Jimmy that she means what she says and that it truly is Jimmy's responsibility, Mom will have to resist the strong desire not to let the cat miss a meal.

Jimmy's response will probably be "When I realized that I forgot, I thought that you would probably feed her." At this point the single parent should reassure the child that the cat is depending on him, and that it is his responsibility to remember.

An older child can be given the experience of accepting a more involved weekly responsibility such as cutting the grass or washing the car. Positive and negative consequences can be coupled with the completion of a responsibility.

Parent: "Jack, you and I have washed the car together now for a long time. It's time for you to take this project on as your own personal responsibility. That means it'll be your responsibility to remember to wash the car each week. I won't be reminding you or nagging you. You must remember on your own. It's really an insult to you when I nag you about something, which I don't want to do. You now have the responsibility to remember that each week the outside of the car will need to be washed and the inside will need to be vacuumed.

"It will need to be done properly before you do anything else on Saturday. That means before you watch television on Saturday or go anywhere, the car must be done. Then I'll be happy to check your job. If you want, you can even do it before Saturday. It is now *your* responsibility, and I want to tell you that I appreciate your help."

Jack will test the seriousness of his mother's commitment to this expectation of responsibility at his first opportunity. He will wonder whether he can get by with a poor job or whether Mom will be willing to make "special" exceptions when he does not get it done. The more consistent the parent is in teaching responsibility, the better the relationship will be between parent and child. Jack will eventually learn that he is really the person who decides how soon he gets to play on Saturday by how soon he gets his responsibility done properly. It will be an experience that will help him to learn not to procrastinate. The lesson will mean extra work in the beginning and sometimes tension for the single parent, but the end result in the child's life will make it worthwhile.

PHASE FOUR: ENCOURAGEMENT

When a single parent gives a child chores to perform around the house, the parent is also arranging for herself opportunities to praise the child. There will be days when Fluffy does not get fed properly or days that Jack must be sent back many times to complete the job. There will also be days, however, when Jack puts forth extra effort and does a good job, or a job that is completed one day early. On these occasions the single parent's response to her child is more important than at any other time.

> *Parent:* "You know, Jack, as a single parent I am very busy. This job you did on the car today is a tremendous help to me, and you did such a good job. Thank you! I'll be proud to have people see me in this car since you've cleaned it so well!"

Whether he is an adolescent or a child, Jack needs to hear these things said to him. A busy single parent can easily forget to let a child know how valuable and cherished he is regardless of what he does. Such positive contributions from the child can act as reminders for the parent to praise the child, making a child feel more like part of the family.

A single parent should take full advantage of this opportunity to praise. When a friend visits and Jack is in the room, the parent might say,

"I'm sure that you noticed how clean my car is today. That's because Jack is now in charge of washing it each week. Didn't he do a great job?" As corny as that may sound, it will go a long way toward reinforcing Jack's good feelings about himself. Though a single parent may not see the gratitude on the child's face, she can be assured that it is in his heart.

Teaching a child to accept responsibility should not be coupled only with negative consequences. The praise and the encouragement are far more important. Ultimately, the child must choose which of these is more significant to him. Praise carries a lot more weight than any punishment or harsh words. Praising a child will teach him how to act in a responsible manner. Criticism alone shows a child how not to do something.

IN REVIEW
Principles for Teaching Responsibility
1. Assigning regular chores gives a child the chance to function as a valuable team member in the family.
2. A chore becomes a responsibility when the child begins to remember to do the chore *without being nagged.*

3. A child has become responsible when he learns to complete the chore.

HITTING HOME

1. As a single parent, do you set the tone by accomplishing the tasks to which you have assigned yourself in the home?
2. Do you take the time to do chores with the child even though you could do them alone much faster?
3. Do you allow your child the freedom to complete a given task within a mutually agreed upon time and without nagging him? Is the task truly *his* responsibility?
4. Does your child know by your response when he has done a good job accepting responsibility?

16

Handling Money

"Johnny acts as if he can turn money off and on like a spigot," Lorraine complained about her fourteen-year-old son. "He simply has no understanding of finances! As soon as Johnny gets a dollar, he spends it and is back for more." With this complaint, Lorraine, a single parent, was asking how to train her son to treat money in a more responsible manner.

Two questions were asked of Lorraine. First of all, did she give, or allow Johnny to earn, a regular weekly allowance? Lorraine's response to this question was "I don't have enough money to give him an allowance." Further investigation revealed that Lorraine handed out money to her son the same way many single mothers do.

Some weeks when Johnny asked for money, she would say "No," because in her opinion there was not enough to pay the bills as it was. Usually a big argument would take place so that the next time Johnny asked her for money she would give him more than she should. It would depend more on her mood than on the budget. If Lorraine felt pressured one week by the bills, then no money was given to Johnny. The next week she might feel guilty about the previous week's argument or about one of many other things concerning her child. On these occasions Johnny was given more spending money than Lorraine could afford to give. The final balance showed that this single mother was sporadically giving her son far more money than she would if she were giving him a regular weekly allowance.

Johnny was not at all responsible for budgeting his money. He was responsible for spending it whenever he could get it. Johnny was also being taught that the bigger the arguments when he did not get the money he asked for, and the more he could make his mother feel guilty, then the better chance he stood of getting money next time. This attitude was not completely Johnny's fault. It was what Lorraine was teaching her son. She was reinforcing the arguments and teaching Johnny how to manipulate her rather than how to handle money.

The second question this single mother had to face was how well she handled budgeting her own finances. What kind of example did she set for her son in the area of handling money?

PHASE ONE: EXAMPLE

It was obvious by the way Lorraine handled her son's allowance that she had no plan of her own for handling money. Johnny was basically acting just like his mother.

What about help from child support? The percentage of noncustodial parents who continue paying the full child support more than a year after the divorce has been reported to be as low as 7 percent. In a questionnaire I handed out to 700 single parents at a weekend retreat, 75 percent of these custodial parents responded by saying that the family income had dropped by more than one-third since the divorce.

Christopher Jenks, a professor of sociology at Northwestern University, found that nine out of ten single mothers experience a 50-percent drop in income. When coupled with the fact that the earning power of women today is still only 57 percent of their male counterparts, Jenkins notes that the families headed by single mothers generally suffer severe economic hardships for several years after the divorce.

"Example! How can I show my child an example of how to budget money? My paycheck is spent as soon as I get it." This was Lorraine's reasoning concerning a budget. She felt she did not make enough to have a budget. That could not have been farther from the truth. It is not only the wealthy who need to have budgets. People not earning enough money to pay their bills are in even more need of a financial plan. Lorraine had to sit down with someone who could help her examine her financial situation—a pastor, close friend, an accountant in the church, and so on.

No magic answers could be given to Lorraine to make her instantly debt free. Having a month-by-month plan, however, did help her become more anxiety free. Simply having a budget was a big help. In her new plan, some bills were paid regularly. Apology letters were sent out to some of her creditors, relating the haphazard way she had handled debts in the past. She also went on to say that though her checks would be smaller, they would now be coming on a regular monthly basis. A number of items Lorraine paid for monthly, such as cable television or eating at fast food restaurants. She decided that expenses like these were not necessities, so she cut them out of her budget.

Getting organized with a planned budget did many things for Lorraine's home. A budget established a financial priority list for her. The single parent now felt comfortable about what needed to be paid and when. Lorraine did much less "binge" spending (going for weeks without buying anything and then buying something that is financially way out of reach).

The budget also helped this single parent deal more objectively with the requests of the children. Whenever a child would ask permission to buy something, Lorraine and her child would look at the balance in the budget book. Together they could see if different items could be afforded. Under this new financial plan the situation was less Lorraine-against-the-children and more a what-can-we-afford time. The responsibility of the final decision was less Lorraine's and more the family's and the budget book's.

The financial plan did more than help stop arguments, however. Lorraine was now setting an example for her children to follow. Johnny was able to see that his mother was no longer living from day to day financially. She was now planning for the family's future. Lorraine was also now giving her children an allowance.

PHASE TWO: EXPOSURE

So often single parents wonder why their children—when they are never exposed to a consistent opportunity—do not know how to handle money wisely. The key to successful training is the way in which the allowance is handled. In order to prepare a child for the way he will need to receive and pay out money in his adult life, a consistent payment plan must be established. A child should receive an allowance on the same day each week and not before or after.

Initially children will take their dollar on Friday afternoon and spend it on the first thing they see. By the next morning the child is once again in poverty and back asking for more. This failure on his part to make his money last the week is an important lesson for the single parent to allow to take place.

> *Parent:* "I'm sorry that you've spent all of your allowance, Son. As I told you when I gave you your allowance, this money must last you until next Friday. Just as I must budget my paycheck to last from week to week—without going to my boss to ask for an advance—so must you."

Under these conditions it will not take long before the child learns that the allowance will be given only on one specific day each week. He will soon realize that it is his responsibility to learn how to make the money last. It is worth repeating that the key to the success of this particular exposure stage of training is *consistency*.

If a parent hands a child money any time the parent feels like it, then the parent is taking on the responsibility of the child's budget. On the other hand, if the child receives money in a regulated, consistent manner, then he learns that it is his responsibility to make the funds last until the next allowance. It is all a matter of who is taking on the responsibility—the single parent or the child. Far too often, single parents rob their children of this opportunity to learn.

An organized training approach such as this should also help limit daily arguments about money. The children may still come back and ask for more, but they already know the answer. That never seems to deter them from testing the system, however. The response is that the parent will be glad to give them the allowance—next Friday. These arguments help focus the responsibility back on the child.

A personal weekly allowance can be very useful in helping a child make realistic decisions about material things that he or she really wants. Many times children just think they "need" the things they see. My experience of walking with my daughter, Torrey, one morning in a shopping center proved that to me. Torrey saw a T-shirt in a window that she "had" to have and indicated that she "would do anything for it." My response to her was "If you think you really want that shirt, I'll drive us back home, and you can take some money out of your little bank. Then we can come back to the store and you can buy it."

She was still excited as we left the shopping area; but as we neared our home, Torrey slowly changed her mind. As we walked into the house, my daughter decided she really did not want the shirt. She "needed" it if I was going to buy it, but if she had to spend her own money on it, she really did not want it. This was a more difficult lesson for me than for her. The T-shirt cost only six dollars, and I could have easily purchased it for her. It would have been worth six dollars to me just to see my daughter's eyes light up. But that would have been serving my needs rather than hers. Several times since then we have seen the shirt. Though I have been tempted to buy it, she hardly gives it a glance. It was a good lesson for both of us.

A single parent faces problems like this regularly, especially when it comes to fad clothing. Much of the time, the single parent, motivated by guilt where her child is concerned, will purchase her child a pair of name-brand designer jeans when the price is way beyond the family's means. One single parent I know about is happy to purchase a pair of regular blue jeans for her child. If the child prefers the expensive name-brand style, the child must pay the difference between the no-name jeans and the expensive designer jeans.

The exposure stage for finances is important as a child begins to handle money. This is the time to be flexible in talking to the children about what to do with their allowance. Training a child about tithing can never start too early in life. Tithing goes hand in hand with the developing of a philosophy of life.

From my own experience, initiating tithing when I was already an adult proved to be very difficult. At twenty-two I felt that I did not have enough money each week for myself, let alone to give some of it to a church. Not having been taught about tithing as a child, I did not realize that tithing is not just giving something that is mine, but rather it is returning just a part of something that has been given to me. A church is not truly the recipient of a tithe. Instead, a tithe is a very small token representing one's relationship to God. In a world that holds wealth at so high a premium, tithing can help a child put things in their proper perspective. If a child is taught to tithe from the time he first receives an allowance, by the time he is an adult, it will have become a way of life.

To get into the habit of saving money on a regular basis is also a subject to be taught during this exposure phase. Saving is a lesson in delayed gratification—postponing a present satisfaction for a future good. Today's world encourages people to be willing to go into debt and have the desired item now. Children will quite naturally succumb to that philosophy.

Saving money in order to purchase something in the future does not come easily in this era of instant coffee, instant meals (microwave-style), and instant financing. It is a lesson that must be taught. Though a parent could easily purchase many of the "wanted" items as opposed to "needed" items, a great lesson is taught when a child tastes the pride of owning something he has bought with his own money.

In the single-parent home where the non-custodial parent will be seeing the child on weekends, this area of training can be difficult. The feeling of saving toward a desired item may be a great accomplishment, but if a child can convince his noncustodial parent on the weekend that the new home video game is a necessity, the whole lesson could go out the window.

Often the noncustodial parent is working through guilt about parenting. He [or she] feels that he must prove to the child that he is still a caring parent and thus makes every weekend they are together like Christmas. There will be more on this topic in the chapter on visitation, but one more idea can be added at this point. If communication between the two "ex-parents" is possible, then it would be advantageous to the child's training to make the noncustodial parent aware of the lesson on saving.

> *Single custodial parent:* "Johnny is working hard at saving money to buy a new video cartridge. I know that either one of us could buy it for him, but if we did that, we would be robbing him of the opportunity to learn about saving toward a goal. Please help me with this. If we could both resist his inevitable begging, then he could feel the pride of buying it for himself."

Maybe the noncustodial parent could contribute to the savings project by allowing the child to earn a little extra doing a job for him during the child's stay. All families are different. This request may work or it may be taken as a challenge by the noncustodial parent. However, the more consistent the training program is, the more thoroughly the lessons will be learned.

PHASE THREE: EXPERIENCE

A family I know planned a vacation about six months in advance. The vacation time spent together was to last for almost one month as the family toured parts of the East Coast. Each of the three teenagers (twelve, fifteen, and sixteen years old) was challenged, six months in advance, to save as much money as he or she could before the vacation. The parent said that he would then match whatever they had saved and that would be their spending money for the trip. The only stipulation was that this money had to be used for any snacks or souvenirs that each child might want. The children were also responsible to pay for their lunches each day.

This experience was a tremendous training opportunity. The children saved anywhere from $100 for the youngest to $220 for the oldest. They cut lawns, washed cars, saved birthday money, and did anything else they could to save money.

The oldest boy decided that he did not want to take all $220 because he had worked hard for it; he felt that he could get along on less money (lesson number one).

For the first time in their lives the children were interested in where they ate lunch because of the price (lesson number two).

The youngest child had a hard time making ends meet and asked one day: "Dad, this is hard. Do you have to save your money for so long so that we can go on vacations?" (lesson number three). By the last week of the trip this same child had spent his money and did not have enough money for lunches. A family meeting was held to discuss the financial problem that the youngest was facing. Every member of the family agreed to take turns paying for lunches for this youngest child during the last few days of the vacation. The looks that this young child received from his older brother and sister reinforced the lesson on budgeting that he needed to learn (lesson number four). The siblings had worked hard for their money and worked even harder not to spend it too quickly. They wanted to be sure that the younger brother was aware of that. The older brother and sister also learned something about bearing the burden for their family (lesson number five).

Children can experience handling money in various ways. Some single parents give their children their lunch money a week in advance and make them responsible for making it last. Another parent I know of has established for his children a "home checking account." Using some old unused checks from a previous bank account, the children write checks when they need some of their money. This parent keeps the allowance and adds it to each child's previous balance every week. The children keep their own balance, and when they want some of their money, they write Mom a fictitious check and she gives them cash.

This process may take a minute or so more, but the children are learning how to keep a balance, as well as how adults handle their money.

Children need many opportunities to experience being responsible for money and the decisions that go with it. At times the child will seem to make bad decisions and spend his money on frivolous items. These are necessary freedoms, however. Only when the child continues to make frivolous decisions or unwise purchases should the parent step in and once again help the child more closely with his money. On the other hand, when the child is doing some good things with his money—such as saving, tithing, and gift giving, the fourth phase should not be forgotten.

PHASE FOUR: ENCOURAGEMENT

Many enticements bombard us everyday. Advertisements are constantly wooing us all into believing that if we purchase this new car or that article of clothing, our lives will experience untold excitement. In the often mundane life of the single parent, these lures can be very enticing indeed. The same holds true for children.

For a child, saving money is boring and the rewards are far away. That is why a parent needs to let the child know how proud she is of her child's decision to save. This kind of reinforcement helps tide him over.

Tithing is another area which gives a child little personal gratification. A parent should make the child aware of the various ministries that he is supporting by his tithe to the church. Training a child in the long-term gratification exemplified by saving or tithing should also include some short-term encouragement from the parent.

One final example about financial training takes me back to my own childhood. My father was a single parent for a certain period of his life, and felt that finances and budgeting were among the most important areas of child training. He would say that a man could ruin his life and future if he did not have a mature attitude toward money. Financial responsibility was so important to him that he had a method that he used to help train me and my brother.

Prior to January, I would write out a request for my allowance and state whether I felt I deserved an increase or not. Next, I was to defend in written form why I wanted the increase, what I was going to do with this allowance, and finally, what I would do to get this allowance. I would then have to submit my request to him. At a later date, he would call me up to his room to defend my request. At the time it seemed very grueling. I know now, however, that it was part of his training plan to teach me about the seriousness of being responsible for money.

To this day, I am very grateful for the way he diligently and painstakingly taught me how to manage my money, and then gave me the opportunity to do it. When he cosigned for me for my first car and told me not to miss a payment, I knew he was serious. There was no doubt in my mind that as much as it might have hurt him, his training would include allowing the bank to repossess my car, rather than his paying my bills for me. Twenty years later my father handed me one of my written allowance requests that he had saved all these years. When my father was a single parent he was extremely busy, but not too busy to train us in areas he thought were important.

IN REVIEW
Principles for Teaching Financial Responsibility
1. Example
   The single parent must use her personal finances in a responsible manner.
2. Exposure
   A child needs an allowance for which he is responsible even if family funds are low.

3. Experience

As a child shows maturity in handling money, he should be given more responsibility in that area.

4. Encouragement

The single parent should be aware of the child's positive actions such as saving money and tithing, and should reinforce this behavior.

HITTING HOME

What is the training plan that I intend to use?

1. What aspects of my financial picture are good? Bad?
2. In what areas do I tend to waste money: entertainment, clothing, food?
3. Am I giving my children an allowance?
4. Am I giving them the chance to develop responsibility in handling finances?
5. Am I encouraging my children to save money? Tithe?
6. Do I encourage them when they make wise purchases, as well as when they save or tithe their money?

17

Visitation

An underlying premise throughout this book has been that the optimum growth of a child results when the rules are consistent. In such an environment a child feels more secure and able to cope. But single parents who want to do the best for their children come against what seems to be an almost insurmountable difficulty.

"What good does it do my child if I spend all week helping him to follow my plan for our home? On weekends his other parent has no rules for him to follow whatsoever!" This lament is typical, and has made many single parents question whether there should be any visitation rights at all for the noncustodial parent. "It brings so much inconsistency into my child's life when he spends a weekend with his dad," a single mother recently told me.

While other single parents may feel the same way, sometimes that can be an excuse to justify a very different feeling—bitterness. The single parent may actually be saying, "After all their father has done to us, he doesn't *deserve* to see the children." In other words, the right of the noncustodial parent to see the children is challenged in order to punish or get even with the parent.

Even though 90 percent of all custodial parents are female, a single custodial father could easily be saying the same thing about his ex-wife.

As we have already discussed, it is very important to help the young boy or girl to understand that the parent-child relationship has not been severed. The noncustodial parent, usually the father, is still the child's parent.

Visitation is an ongoing opportunity for a child to grow to believe that he was not the cause of the divorce. An opportunity to be with his father is proof for him that he, the child, has not been abandoned. It is also important for a child to know that his father loves him. As many single parents know, the opportunity for making this fact known is not always available. A large percentage of children are never able to be with their father, and the reasons behind this fact must be carefully shared with the child. Left in the dark, the child will certainly fantasize that he is the one responsible for driving Dad out of his life. Sometimes the value of visitation for the sake of the child's self-esteem might well outweigh the difficulties brought on by a lack of structure.

Often both parents involved truly love their child and have this child's best interest as their major concern. Communication between these two separated parents may be possible. Even in situations where a bitter divorce has caused a strain between the parents, conversation for the sake of the child's development is strongly urged. Communication of this nature should focus on the topic of the child and his needs. Ex-spouses must be willing to calmly discuss the child's routine, including appropriate chores and bedtimes. These discussions are not occasions for ultimatums or for heaping guilt on one another.

In his book *Communication: Key to Your Marriage,* H. Norman Wright tells a story about an old man who lived all winter in a cabin on the side of the mountain. He would spend much of his day watching the wildlife in the valley below. One day a herd of wild horses came into the valley to graze. Soon a pack of

wolves appeared and prepared to attack the
horses. As the wolves got closer, the horses
formed a circle with their heads in the center
so that they could kick out at the wolves as
they attacked. This strategy helped the horses
defeat their problem, and the wolves soon
left. A few days later a herd of wild jackasses
roamed into the valley in search of food. The
same pack of wolves appeared and approached
this new prey. As the wolves prepared to attack,
the jackasses circled up. These animals, however, used a different kind of circle. Instead of
facing in toward the center like the horses,
they faced out toward the wolves. As the
wolves attacked them, the jackasses mistakenly
kicked in at each other instead of out at their
attackers.

So often people who are divorced handle
their problems like the jackasses in the story.
Instead of attacking the problem and solving
it, the two parents end up attacking each other
and solving nothing. The problem to be solved
is how to have a consistent environment for
the child when he spends time in two separate
homes. Kicking at this problem will offer opportunities to remedy some of the inconsistencies.
However, kicking at an ex-spouse will only make
future communication more difficult.

Mom: "Billy goes to bed at 8:30 every night. He usually tries to get me to let him stay up later, but I try to be firm. I could really use some help in teaching him the importance of personal discipline, because he is so persistent about dragging out his bedtime."

Dad: "You mean you want me to put him to bed at 8:30 on a weekend?"

Mom: "No, you're right. Since it's a weekend, he should be able to stay up a little later. I need help teaching him to go to bed at a prearranged time that he has been told is his bedtime."

Dad: "Do you think you should be the one to set the bedtime?"

Mom: "No, it's your home, and I think that you should set the time. I just want your help in sticking to the bedtime. With me, Billy, like most children, tries to do little things to make it so that he can stay up past the time he is supposed to go to bed. I'm having a difficult time with this, and we need your help."

This form of communication hits at the problem. Regardless of how difficult one ex-partner may make it to communicate, the other partner must not fall into the trap of hitting back. The main purpose of communication in this instance should always be the child and his consistent training. Discussing other personal matters will only poison opportunities for the child's successful transition from one home to the other.

In some divorce situations, communication is seemingly impossible because of unresolved bitterness and hurt. The parents are not talking to each other and spend much of their energy disapproving of one another's life-style. This tension forces children into an ugly position. The child in the single-parent home where open and expressed bitterness exists can be abused emotionally.

Some parents, custodial and noncustodial alike, attempt to win their child's allegiance by making maligning and judgmental statements about the other parent. Many children of divorced homes must endure a childhood of listening to derogatory comments about that person they call "Daddy." These children are forced not only to listen, but also to take sides. If a child questions the validity of the harsh judgments, he too, may fall under the wrath of a parent. Single parents sometimes get caught in this judgment game because they feel backed into a corner. They may feel the need to justify their innocence in the marital breakup. In order to win the child's allegiance and sympathy, the other parent must be shown to be a villain: "Why did your daddy and I get divorced? Well, ah . . . because this daddy that you seem to love so much did this and that to us."

Adults can choose new spouses, but children are born to one set of parents. Though an insecure single mother may be ridiculing a man she is no longer married to, she is also talking to a child about the daddy that child will have for life. It is very unfair to force a child to feel that he must choose between Mom or Dad. It is putting him in the eye of the storm.

The child can be and often is abused in another way. Some single parents and noncustodial parents use visitation as an opportunity to spy on their ex-spouse. They may not intentionally use the child's weekend as a way to find out how the other parent is living, but they fall into a habit of asking specific questions. The child returns from a weekend with Dad and goes through a routine interrogation:

Mom: "What did you do with your dad this weekend?"

"Did he have beer in his refrigerator?"
"When you went out to eat, was it just the two of you or was there someone else with you?"
"Does he get a lot of phone calls?"
"Did you ever answer the phone and hear who it was?"
"Did you go to church on Sunday?"

The list goes on and on. As the questions move from curiosity to prying, the child can be made to feel as if he is being forced to take sides. How much should he report? Should he tell Mom about things she is not even asking about? The child could easily wonder if the purpose of visitation is for him to report incriminating evidence, rather than to be with his father.

An astute child can turn this abusive situation into an opportunity to manipulate his estranged parents by reporting only the things that will benefit him or his particular wants. The child can thus find stimulation in this new way to get his estranged parents to pay attention to him. Unfortunately, the parents may not be listening to the child, but to the reports about one another. Eventually the parents may become less and less interested in the reports and thus pay less attention to the child. At this point a child may exaggerate the tales he has to tell—all in a desperate attempt to regain the attention of his parent. Now the child is being reinforced for lying. As the child makes up or colors stories about one parent, he receives what he wants more than anything in the world: the undivided attention of his parent.

Even innocent interrogation of a child after a visit with one parent can inject many negatives into the life of the child, who is forced to take sides and to pass judgments on one of his parents. The attention he receives for reporting the gossip can, in some cases, encourage him to manipulate and eventually lie. The single parent who truly loves such a child will respond: "That's your father's business. Yes, I know you tell me that he asks you many questions about me, but I think I would prefer not to have you report those things to me. He's an adult and able to make his own decisions." Statements like this can discourage the child from gossiping, exaggerating, or spying for attention. The single parent can also be saved from hearing things that may cause unnecessary pain. Visitation should have the positive purpose of giving a child time to be with his other parent.

Many hurts and pains accompany visitation. During the week, life at home is filled with school, chores, and other mundane things. Life on the weekends with Dad, however, is often like vacation time and going to Disneyland. Single custodial parents may feel the need to compete with the noncustodial parent. However, the single parent should swallow hard and consider all the opportunities her child is being given: "Isn't it nice that you have a dad that can do all of those things with you?" Statistics and studies tell us that the "Disneyland weekends" do not last very long anyway; thus the child should be allowed to enjoy them and share them with his mother if he cares to.

A single parent reading this chapter may say, "How can I be sweet and endure the abusive things that my ex says about me to my child? What will my child think if I don't defend myself?" It is the final outcome or development of the child that is the basic concern. As the child grows older, he will easily be able to discern the difference between a bitter, vindictive parent and a forgiving, loving parent.

These two contrasting attitudes had a major impact in my own life. While I was in undergraduate school in East Tennessee, a local pastor spent some of his time talking to me about spiritual things. He was a very loving and kind man with a strong faith in Christ. I was not a Christian at that time, so I listened to what he had to say more out of politeness than anything else. At about the same time, an outspoken atheist came to my college campus to speak. Excited about the opportunity to hear this nationally known figure, I went to one of her talks. What she had to say caught me off guard. Never in my life had I heard such bitterness pour from one individual. She stood at the podium condemning and cursing churches, preachers, and anything related to God. Toward the end of her address, I leaned back in my chair and suddenly saw my pastor friend leaning against the back wall of the auditorium. He was a huge man, cut from the hard mountain stock of East Tennessee, and yet as I looked at him more closely, I could not believe what I saw. Tears were streaming down his face. As he looked at the abusive speaker, it was not with bitterness, but with compassion.

That night in my dorm room alone, I sat thinking about the contrast. One person had been contemptuously cursing everything that the other person stood for. Yet the other person had not responded with hate or anger, but with love and compassion. Though the girl I had been dating (and eventually married) had been talking to me about Christ, I had not been able to picture his love for me. That vivid contrast in attitudes was the final straw that caused me to make my decision for Christ. The contrast between love and hate was so strong that I could easily see the difference, and I knew which way I wanted to live.

Many single parents may be in the same position. Because of their faith or their positive attitude, they may be under a constant barrage of ridicule from an ex-spouse. The important thing for the child to see is that this ridicule does not elicit a response in kind. Much more of an impact will eventually be made when the contrast in attitudes is obvious. I will never forget how that minister responded to that atheist's ridicule with true forgiveness and love. When he grows older, the child in the single-parent home will not forget what he has seen either.

IN REVIEW

Principles of Visitation

1. Visitation should give a child an opportunity to get to know his noncustodial parent.

2. Visitation should help a child realize that he was not divorced, but rather that it was his parents who got divorced.
3. Each parent must be on guard against emotionally abusing a child by using visitation for other personal reasons.
4. The custodial parent must depend on Christ's strength to sustain her through the strains brought on by visitation.

18

Blending Two Families

In 1965 my father announced to me and my brother, Steven, that after having been a single parent for quite a while, he was getting remarried. I was sixteen, and Steven had just turned eleven. We had come to know this lady since we had spent time with her, but I do not believe either of us ever imagined that my father would remarry. A long time after our mother's death, he had started dating, often bringing us with him on different outings. That was great for all of us. The thought of someone actually moving in and becoming Mrs. Barnes, however, was very hard for me to comprehend. Steven and I had so many questions about this new step-parent relationship that we were about to experience. No matter how I looked at it, however, my biggest concern was how this new relationship in our home would affect my old relationship with my father. Would he love me any less when he remarried?

Children often view love as a commodity or quantity rather than as a quality. With this perspective, it would seem natural to imagine that my father had only a certain amount of love in his bucket. As a child, I assumed he would have to take back some of it in order to give it to his new wife. After all, he had only so much love in that imaginary bucket to give out.

The concept of love is very difficult for even adults to understand. For a child struggling with his own personal worth and lovableness, the whole concept is mind-boggling. As the stepparent enters the home, the natural reaction of the child is to be jealous. I can remember feeling that my new stepmother had come into our lives to take Dad away from us.

It has been said that children tend to spell *love* as T-I-M-E. A parent can say anything he wants to or even buy anything for the child, but deep down inside, the child knows that if his parent wants to spend time with him, it is proof of his love. Time is the commodity in short supply. A parent may say that she does not have enough money to do something, but she can always borrow or charge the purchase that she desires. Not so for time.

Time forces everyone to put things into priority order. We may not truly believe that the things we do are more important than the things we postpone. The fact that one thing is chosen over another, however, indicates that a priority decision has been made. This is not always true because we are sometimes forced into spending our time doing things that do not necessarily hold a priority position in our lives. What we do with our time does at least give a hint to those around us of the things we have set aside as top priorities.

The child measures love in a very similar way. When one of my children sees me playing with a sibling, often the first one will run to us, as if to make sure she gets her share of time or love. Children believe that time is given to the object or thing that is loved the most. If the child finds it difficult to get the attention of his single parent, he may assume that it will be even harder to spend time with his mother when another factor, her new husband, is brought into the picture. The fear of losing the love of a parent is a real crisis in the child's life. Very little can be done to bring instant relief to this anguish. There are logical explanations such as "Now that I am married and there are two parents running this family, it will help me have more time to spend with you, Son." Another attempt to reassure the child is "I was so lonely before I got remarried, but now that I am married I am so much happier. It helps me to be better able to meet your needs and be a better mom." All of that may be true, but to the child, another person in the home or another whole family only means that he has got to share his single parent.

The eventual cure for this anxiety lies with an awareness and sensitivity on the part of the newly married parent. After a period of time in which the child learns to understand the new arrangement, the child can grow to realize that he has not lost a mom, but instead has gained a dad. When two families are "blending," the child's overall thought is "Am I losing or gaining by this situation? Will I lose Mom and some of her love?"

WHO GOT MARRIED IN THIS DEAL?

While talking with a teenaged boy from a recently blended family, I heard him repeatedly

use the phrase, "My mother's husband." I
asked him who his mother's new husband was
to him. What was his relationship to this new
man in his family? The boy could not verbalize
how he felt he and his mother's husband fit
together. When he could not respond, I asked
him, "What do you call him when you talk to
him?" His response showed the awkwardness
of his dilemma. "I just don't call him anything.
If I don't have his attention, I just wait until he
is looking right at me."

This encounter instantly reminded me of
two similar occasions in my own life. The
most recent of the two was when I had visited
my in-laws for the first time after my marriage. I knew that the marriage ceremony
had brought my wife and me into the same
family, but I was not sure how it affected my
relationship with her parents. A difficult situation for me was what I should call her father.
What title should I use? How should I address
him? I was not really his son so I might be
encroaching on sacred ground to refer to him
as "Dad."

Ten years later, after avoiding using a title
when I talked to my father-in-law, I finally got
the courage to assume it would be all right to
start calling him "Dad." The first few attempts

at saying "Dad" were extremely awkward, but after feeling that there were no objections, I kept on until I was more comfortable. Many sons-in-law avoid this situation all together by waiting until they have children. Then they begin referring to their father-in-law as "Granddad."

The other time in my life when I had to deal with the problem of what label to use was when my single parent remarried. I knew that this woman had married my father, but had she married his children also? Were we part of the ceremony? Unfortunately, the topic was never discussed, so for years I called this adult lady by her first name. I often felt ridiculous because at that time I knew no other adult to whom I referred on a first-name basis. Just because this nice lady had moved into our home had not been enough.

A strange phenomenon often takes place when two families blend to make one. First, the parents marry, and the two groups move into the same house. From that point until the first crisis, there is little or no communication. Everyone feels his way through the family-blending process as if testing a newly frozen lake. Far too many things are assumed. Only when a crisis between family members takes place is communication forced.

THE EXECUTIVE STAFF MEETING

The first step toward a successful blend is to open the lines of communication between the parent and the stepparent. Each adult must know what the other adult feels is the primary relationship in the home. The husband and the wife must reassure each other that they are truly trying to become one. The primary relationship in the family is the marriage bond. Through a positive, communicating marital relationship, the two parents can better meet the needs of their most important ministry—the children.

Communicating parents can give each other "permission to parent" the children. It is very basic and extremely important that each parent know that he or she is expected to train and to get involved in the lives of the other parent's children. Disciplinary guidelines must be discussed and established so that both parents can strive to respond to the needs of the children in the same, consistent manner. Being open and frank, especially about feelings and insecurities over the way the children are responding, is important during these staff meetings.

Mother: "It seems to me that you've been responding to Tommy in a very cold manner lately."

Stepfather: "I want to tell you it's not true, but I can't. It seems to me that Tommy is trying to cause problems just to drive a wedge between you and me."

Mother: "I hadn't thought about it like that, but you may be right. I do know this, however; it can never happen unless we let it happen. As long as you and I are able to be as open as we are now, we will be able to show Tommy that we are going to remain a family forever."

It is important to hold "executive staff meetings" at least weekly so that the list of problems does not become insurmountable. Difficulties between stepparent and child must be discussed as soon as possible, before they drive a wedge into the marital relationship.

Each parent should also be prepared to fight the urge to intervene between the other parent and the child during disciplinary actions and discussions. Such silent support is crucial. A single parent may have spent years as her child's only protector. A single mother may have conditioned herself to overprotect her "cub" from the harsh world. When she remarries and the child decides to test his mother's new husband, everyone is caught in a priority dilemma. The child wonders whether this new man will care enough to do what he has said he will do. The stepfather wonders whether his new wife means what she says by wanting him to become a parent to her child. Will she support him or will she return to her protector role and come between them?

The former single parent has the most difficult, yet the most significant, decision to make. "Is my husband being too harsh as he makes his first attempt at being a parent? How will my son respond when I do not come to his rescue this time? Will my son understand that I will not intervene because I love him?" These are significant questions, but the most significant of all is "What can I do to make the greatest impact for the greatest good as far as my husband and my child are concerned?"

If the child's mother comes to the child's "rescue," the stepfather is forced to adopt one of two approaches. One option for the stepfather is to decide that it is just not worth it. Why try to reprimand the child only to end up losing the battle and risking a disagreement with his new wife? This approach would be one of avoiding all future parental duties that may prove to be controversial.

A second option that a stepfather might take would be to overcompensate. Since the child's mother intervened, the stepfather becomes even harsher in disciplining the child. In his mind this is done to balance the scales that the mother is trying to tilt. She lets the child escape punishment; so out of frustration, the husband uses more severe punishment. This whole cycle has little to do with the child. He is only being used as each parent displays frustration in their attitude toward this child. In this atmosphere, conditions get worse and worse until they grow to crisis proportions.

Communication that is scheduled on a regular, ongoing basis can help this problem be avoided. Criticism of each other's handling of the child should be conducted only in the privacy of "executive meetings." To argue about him, in front of him, can only perpetuate his old feelings that he might have been the cause of the divorce: "Now look what's happening; I'm causing another marriage to fall apart." The honest communication that takes place in the executive staff meetings will help give the child a secure home as the two people responsible for the leadership in his home are able to work together. The newly married couple can pull the child along in the same direction rather than pulling him apart because of poor communication.

FAMILY MEETINGS

Communication helps the two parents establish a common direction. Each parent gives the other parent permission to help train the children, and when this has happened it is time to announce the direction to the children. This Family Meeting is a time to apprise the children of what their new relationships in the blended family are all about.

Mother: "Earl and I have decided that we would set this evening aside to discuss our new family with you."

Tommy: "What are we going to talk about, Mom?"

Mother: "Tonight, we want to discuss how each of us fits into this home as we blend our two families together. Earl is going to be the father of our home, and that means we'll all be following his leadership. I've asked him to treat all the children in this house the same. Tommy, that means that he will be loving you and disciplining you just as he does Linda and Bobby."

Earl: "Tommy, I'm not here to try to make you forget your father. That should never happen. I'm here because I love your mom, and when I married her I married you, too. I'm excited to have you as a new son, and I'll try to help you just as if I've known you forever. I know that I'll make mistakes, and I want you to come and talk with me when you think that I'm not being fair. Remember this: loving someone means being his friend, and it also means helping him be the best person he can possibly be. We'll have to do that for each other. Do you have anything you want to ask me?"

Tommy: "Well, what name do you want me to call you? Before you and Mom got married, I called you Uncle Earl. That seems kind of funny now."

Earl: "What you call me is up to you. If you would like to, I would be honored if you called me 'Dad.' I know I'm not your father so that might be hard at first, but it's really up to you. If you would be more comfortable, you could call me Earl."

Tommy: "Mom, what should I do?"

Mother: "That's up to you, Tommy. If you

call Earl 'Dad,' it doesn't mean that you have taken anything away from your real father. It means you're kind of lucky to have two dads. But Earl said it was up to you."

Family meetings teach children to begin to express honest feelings. Many children from single-parent homes suppress their true feelings for a variety of reasons. One obvious reason is that they do not know how to talk about their feelings. For example, whenever they did express true feelings, their single parent got too emotional. Under the new circumstances of a blended family, the child can be encouraged to talk as he sees his new "Dad" express how he feels about things. Communication is a major ingredient in successful family blending. It will not happen unless the new family structures the meetings into their routine.

The family meetings will also help the child to understand the mechanics of his new family. He wants to know how it operates and who is in charge. That is another major question to the child. The family meeting gives him the opportunity to hear about the family structure, but hearing is not always the same as believing. Once the communication has taken place, the child may want to test the new structure to find out if it really works.

When the testing time takes place, husband and wife must do more than function as a consistent unit. They must also *encourage* each other.

Mother: "Thanks for handling Tommy the way you did today. It was so encouraging to see you correct him, and then try to lift his spirits later on."

Stepfather: "Thanks for saying that. I was a little uncomfortable about reprimanding Tommy with you standing right there. It seemed that he kept looking for you to save him. I appreciate the way you stayed out of it."

Encouragement! That is another of the all-important ingredients. When handling another person's child, the stepparent is dealing not only with the child. Inside he is also wondering what the child's parent is thinking. Love, communication, and encouragement will help both adults feel more secure in their new roles.

The blended family will spend quite a long period of time learning to understand and adjust to each other. At the same time, however, they can have fun just becoming a family. This new family can begin to develop special traditions and events. Each member takes a turn at being in charge of activities such as game night. One of the younger children might be given the task of choosing the refreshment for a special family night. The adults can alternate spending individual time with each child. Fun activities can help everyone get to know each other.

The actual quest for unity within a family can be a blessing to all involved. It takes time and a willingness to give of oneself. Under these circumstances two families can become blended into one unit, and the lives of all its members can be enhanced in the process. Nothing can be taken for granted, however—neither the love, nor the rules. All the members must be informed of what the merger means to them and to their life-style. A blended family works to help everyone blend, and yet is patient with those who are slow to blend. A blended family, as in all families, will only be as strong as its leadership.

IN REVIEW
Principles for Blending Two Families
1. A blended family should help the children to understand that they are not losing the love of their natural parent.

2. Communication on all levels is essential to a successful blend.
3. Mutual encouragement helps each parent to know he or she is performing correctly.
4. Blending two families should include fun and new family traditions.

19

The Unresponsive Child

Working in a residential setting for teenagers who have not responded to the authority in their own homes, I frequently counsel single parents who have put a tremendous effort into the task of parenting. Many of these single parents have worked with their children from an early age to help them develop a strong Christ-centered philosophy of life. Yet even in such positive and enriched settings, some children do not respond.

For various reasons, some children continually fight and challenge the authority of the most balanced homes. It seems that no matter how consistent and loving the home is, a particular child may display an attitude and a behavior that are constant sources of heartache to his single parent.

Continuing to train the child, this parent may eventually ask the question, "What is left to do for my child since he is not responding to anything?" A first step should be taken in a case like this—seek the help of a pediatrician. Inform him ahead of time of the child's behavioral problems. Because some behavior problems may stem from a physical problem, it is wise for the child to have a complete physical examination.

Years ago my office sent an older adolescent to the doctor to be checked. The child was extremely moody and at times displayed very disruptive behavior. Initially nothing was discovered to be physically wrong with him. After the third set of tests this particular child was discovered to have hypoglycemia. With the help of an endocrinologist the child was put on a special diet. It was amazing how his behavior and moods began to fall back into the "normal" range. Seeing a physician is an important first step when children are not responding to a home and to a parent who provides love and structure.

The majority of nonresponsive children will

not be found to have organic problems. Thus, the second step for the single parent may be to seek emotional help for the child. A counselor or psychologist should be sought—one who meets certain important criteria.

The single parent for whom Christ is central to the family's decisions will want to choose a therapist of the same religious belief. A counselor who is not a Christian may cause further confusion in the home, rather than help to rectify the child's feelings about self and his role within the family unit. However, this is not always the rule, nor is it always possible to find a competent Christian counselor.

Some non-Christian therapists are able to work with Christian families in a way that can offer help and direction. It is important for the single parent to find out early the therapist's feelings about Christianity. Too often clients act as if they work for the counselor and thus have no right to ask questions. This could not be further from the truth!

A counselor is an employee of the client, who should interview the counselor as if the client were deciding whether to hire him or not.

Single Parent: "I am a born-again Christian, and I teach the Christian faith in my home.

How do you feel about this personally? Do you think my faith will hinder you when you counsel with my family?"

It is obvious that the optimum situation would be to work with a qualified, competent counselor who functions with the same basic beliefs as does the single parent.

A second criteria a counselor should meet is a willingness to work with both the family and the child. Children of single-parent homes are still part of a unit called the family. The child with emotional struggles will be able to better integrate himself back into his family if the family is helped to be a better recipient. The single parent and siblings can learn to work together to draw a troubled child back into the nurturing team.

It is also important to select a professional. In today's world many people hang a shingle outside their door and claim to be qualified counselors, when in reality they may do more harm than good. The role or position should not be reversed as if the counselor is doing the selecting. The single parent should feel free to ask questions about the counselor's training and experience, whether the therapist is licensed, whether he is a member of a professional organization, and if he has any references. Quite often pastors are good resource people when it comes to hunting for a qualified, professional counselor.

Getting help for the physical and emotional needs of a troubled child may not be the final answer. A child may still fail to respond to the leadership of the single parent. Some children act as if they are completely untouched by the love around them. Such children may have needs no medical or psychological help can meet. There is, however, another source of help available to the single parent. Too often, as parents we forget that God loves our children far more than we could ever begin to. It is important that every single parent remember she is not raising her child by herself. God is a loving partner in the task of training children. Even when a child seems totally lost, it is the wise single parent who continues to express love to the child and prays for him with the knowledge that God answers prayer.

A mother recently told me about the son she kept praying for:

"From age thirteen on, Fred was in and out of detention homes. When he finally came back home, all he did was continually run away. My family and friends saw that he was breaking my heart and told me to forget about him. They advised me not to let him back in the house. He was breaking my heart; they were right. But I loved him and couldn't just give up on him. All that was left for me to do was to let him know I loved him and prayed for him every day. Fred is seventeen and back home now. At least for the past few months things have been fine. I know it will take more time, but I also know that God answers prayer."

The story in the Gospel of Luke about the loving father (commonly referred to as the "Parable of the Prodigal Son") is a good illustration of a parent who knew he had done all he could, so he confidently waited for his child to turn toward God. In Luke 15:11 Jesus begins to relate the story of a man who had raised two sons. The youngest of the two took all he could get from his father, saying, "I want my share of your estate now, instead of waiting until you die!" (Luke 15:12). Upon receiving the portion he had demanded, he left home and squandered his father's wealth on wild living. This child was probably doing all the things his father had taught him were wrong to do. It was a classic case of rebellion on the child's part.

As the parable comes to a close, we learn two very important things about this boy and his father. The boy eventually realizes he has made a horrible mistake, proving it with this statement in verses eighteen and nineteen: "I will go home to my father and say, 'Father, I have sinned against both heaven and you, and am no longer worthy of being called your son.'" For this son to finally come to this realization means he must have been taught the true meaning of sin. Although he had not obviously responded to the spiritual training he had received in the home, he certainly remembered the lesson. He knew that the life he had been living was a sin against God and against his father. That kind of understanding does not come naturally—it has to be taught. It is obvious that a very responsible parent had lovingly trained his son, even though the son had not responded.

This parable shows us another very important quality of the father. He must have had faith that his son would someday return to the things he had been taught. This is suggested in verse twenty: "So he returned home to his father. And while he was still a long distance away, his father saw him coming, and was filled with loving pity and ran and embraced him and kissed him."

The reader can almost picture the father with his eye on the horizon, knowing that his son would one day return. How could this parent have known that? I believe that the father in this parable could have that kind of assurance for two very significant reasons. He was counting on the way he had raised his son; someday his boy would respond to his loving training. He was also counting on God to honor his Word. "Teach a child to choose the right path, and when he is older, he will remain upon it" (Proverbs 22:6). This verse does not say he will remain upon it when he is an adolescent. It says, "when he is older." The father of this difficult boy was clinging to the promise that God would help him with his child since the child had been trained in the things God had prescribed.

This attitude of assurance is what the single parent of a nonresponsive child must maintain. I am confident that the kind of loving father depicted in Luke prays daily for his wayward child. When all else seems to have failed, the single parent must continue to pray and to train the difficult child in a loving, consistent manner. A parent is responsible to God for the training and nurturing. God alone can truly change a defiant heart.

This parable of a loving father also has another application. It is a picture of God's love for each of us. Regardless of the life-style or waywardness that anyone of us may have displayed in the past, there is our heavenly Father waiting and watching for each of us. At the moment one of God's children is willing to say, "Father, I have sinned against you and I am unworthy," God will wrap his love around his child. The key is that he is waiting with a forgiveness that could come only from perfect love.

When the task of the single parent seems insurmountable, she, too, can look to the Father for help. In the long and lonely journey of training up a child alone, the single parent can find God's strength and direction—even in the face of discouraging odds.

20

No Longer
a Crisis
Parent

When I first arrived at Sheridan House for
Boys, I spent some time talking with my prede-
cessor about the duties of the executive director of this ministry. Driving home from the
office after this conversation, I felt somewhat
discouraged. The day-to-day tasks seemed to
be so immense that I wondered if I would have
enough hours in the day left over to plan for
future development. The job description indicated I would have to spend all my available
time "putting out fires."

The next six months at Sheridan House
proved my expectations correct. I would no
sooner deal with one crisis when I would be

forced to take on another explosive situation. Feeling like a fireman, I was simply putting out one fire after another without having any time to do prevention work. I began to feel that either I was incompetent or the job could not be done.

The sense of being overwhelmed is one shared by many single parents. At the end of a recent weekend seminar on single parenting, a single parent said, "I can certainly see the need to train my child in all of these areas, and now I have a much better understanding of how to train my child. But how in the world do I begin to do it all?" This single mother was expressing her total sense of inadequacy for the task that was before her.

Without question, the responsibility of training a child is an awesome task. There is probably not a parent to be found anywhere who feels totally adequate at parenting. As difficult as parenting is, however, it is more than simply a task to be done. It is a responsibility that all parents must accept as a priority in their lives.

Almost all single parents acknowledge the difficulties involved in dedicating the proper time to parenting. Unfortunately, some parents become so overwhelmed by the task that they back away from parenting and focus on other less demanding responsibilities. For these single parents the fires just keep getting bigger and bigger until their crisis intervention style of parenting gives way to disaster in the home and they completely give up. Fortunately, most single parents accept their responsibility as a priority, no matter how difficult a job it is.

A single parent cannot decide one day to teach everything her children need to learn and then simply step out the next day and accomplish it. That cannot be done no matter how many parents are in a home. Developing a workable, day-to-day plan to "train up a child in the way he should go" (Proverbs 22:6, KJV) takes time and step-by-step planning.

Years ago I decided that it was a must for me to begin jogging to stay in shape. Now that I look back on it, the real reason I wanted to jog was that it was the thing to do—and I certainly wanted to be in vogue. With my motivation all wrong, I began the next day as if I were a jogger. Three miles seemed a reasonable distance for a jogger to run, so I got up at dawn to a new experience. I put on my color-coordinated outfit and trotted out the door to join the ranks of joggers.

Darting down the first street on my three-mile route, I had fantasies of entering the Orange Bowl Marathon. After all, this was only the first day, and I was zipping through my first two hundred yards. Who said distance running was difficult? Surely, it wouldn't take long for me to get up to a distance of twenty-six miles.

As I turned on to a main street, I passed my first half mile, and I began to wonder if that could really have been only a half mile. Maybe I'd made a mistake laying out the course in the car. I pushed on, though, because I was now a jogger. Later (how much later I could no longer estimate), I jogged by the marker I had designated for my first mile. At this point I could no longer feel my feet, and I was gasping for air; but I was determined to push on.

The agony I was going through during my second mile caused people in the passing cars to turn back and stare at me. "Should we pull over to the side and help you or just drive on and call the rescue squad?" their glances indicated. I must have become delirious at some point because I do not remember when I turned off to take a shortcut back to my house. Half an hour of "jogging" brought me back down my street. By this time my pace was slower than if I had been on my hands and knees. When I reached my front lawn, that is exactly what happened. I fell to my hands and knees and threw up just in time for a friend to drive up and ask me what I was doing. Gasping, I replied in a very unfriendly voice, "I'm jogging."

Obviously my embarrassing story illustrates how *not* to attempt a life-changing project. It cannot be done all in one day, but instead it takes small steps combined with a long-term commitment. After calling in sick that day, I later learned from a friend that joggers tackle one block at a time!

Single parenting also begins one "block" at a time. The first block or step is to check the philosophy of life being exemplified in the home. Does the single parent truly place Christ as the top priority and set aside time for family devotions? This is the first and most important aspect to be mastered. As the family's spiritual growth is underway, then and only then should another "block" be added to the run.

There comes a time when training areas can be combined or taught together. For instance, a discussion time of the rules and discipline can help the child to feel that his opinion is valued. During these discussions a child can further develop his communication skills. He can also learn to feel better about himself. Like jogging, this training takes time and practice. None of it will ever happen, however, if the single parent does not begin the journey. Long, and often lonely, the journey must be taken one step at a time. For those willing to go through the effort, however, the end results outweigh the agony.

I "jogged" for only a month or so because my motivation had been wrong in the first place. My primary motivation to run had not been out of devotion to God. In fact, I had never even discussed my jogging with God. I was going to jog because it "seemed like the thing to do."

Our contemporary society says as much about developing yourself. "Be number one, rather than spend time developing your children." Fortunately, the pendulum is starting to swing back toward family values, but parents, and especially the single parent, still have a strong tide to buck.

It will take special strength and fortitude for a single parent to dedicate herself to training her children. That strength comes as she seeks God's wisdom and support on a daily basis. A growing faith in Christ and making a relationship with him the top priority—these are the motivating forces that will endure.

A similar commitment motivated Moses to return to Egypt to lead the children of Israel. Prior to his return, Moses had protested: "But I'm not the person for a job like that." What he was really saying was that he lacked the necessary skills to parent all those complaining "children." God did not disagree with Moses. Recognizing that Moses was inadequate for the task, God promised, "I will certainly be with you" (Exodus 3:12). That assurance was all Moses needed to go from failure in his own abilities to confidence in what the Lord could do through him. There is a lesson here for single parents to remember for themselves.

But how does a single parent stop being a crisis parent? First, she prays and works hard to develop a suitable plan for her family—one that honors God. Then the single parent takes the second step and begins parenting in a consistent manner.

When one day does not seem to work out right, she doesn't give up. The next day she continues her journey as a single parent. Most importantly, as a single parent she dedicates herself to trying to parent with God as her Motivator. The children will not necessarily say "thank you." Their response to the parenting process will often only discourage the single parent. For this reason she must depend upon God for encouragement.

The second wilderness journey for Moses was at best a very difficult period of time. His children, the Israelites, spent much of their energy complaining, but great things still happened along the way. For the single parent, the second wilderness journey comes as she walks her child into adulthood. It, too, is filled with difficulties. Like the Exodus, her journey may often seem to be running in circles without clear purpose. With God and his plan in the forefront, however, the single parent can overcome the wilderness. The journey through it is accomplished one step at a time, one day after another, hand in hand with her children and the presence of the Lord to lead the way.

Suggested Reading

Chapter Two

Stewart, Suzanne. *Parent Alone*. Waco, Texas: Word Books, 1978.

Vigeveno, H. S. and Claire, Anne. *Divorce and the Children*. Glendale, California: Regal Books, 1979.

Watts, Virginia. *The Single Parent*. Old Tappan, New Jersey: Fleming H. Revell Co., 1979.

Chapter Three

Hyder, O. Q. *The Christian's Handbook of Psychiatry*. Old Tappen, New Jersey: Fleming H. Revell Co., 1971.

Welter, Paul. *How to Help a Friend*. Wheaton, Illinois: Tyndale House Publishers, Inc., 1978.

Chapter Six
Christensen, Larry. *The Christian Family*. Minneapolis, Minnesota: Bethany Fellowship, 1970.

Chapter Eight
Campbell, Ross. *How to Really Love Your Child*. Wheaton, Illinois: Victor Books, 1977.
Elder, Carl. *Values and Moral Development in Children*. Nashville, Tennessee: Broadman Press, 1976.
Sunukjian, Donald. *You Can Help Your Child Grow*. Dallas, Texas: Dallas Seminary Literature Ministry.

Chapter Nine
Briggs, Dorothy Corkville. *Your Child's Self-esteem*. Garden City, New York: Dolphin Books, 1975.
Dobson, James. *Dr. Dobson Answers Your Questions*. Wheaton, Illinois: Tyndale House Publishers, Inc., 1982.
_____*Hide or Seek*. Old Tappen, New Jersey: Fleming H. Revell Co., 1974.
Francke, Linda Bird. *Growing Up Divorced*. New York: Linden Press, 1983.
Narramore, Bruce. *Help, I'm a Parent*. Grand Rapids, Michigan: Zondervan Publishing Co., 1972.

Chapter Ten

Ackerman, Paul and Kappelman, Murray. *Signals*. New York: Dial Press, 1978.

Chafin, Kenneth. *Is There a Family in the House?* Waco, Texas: Word Books, 1978.

Gaylin, Willard. *Caring*. New York: Alfred A. Knopf Co., 1976.

Powell, John. *Why Am I Afraid to Tell You Who I Am?* Allen, Texas: Argus Communications, 1969.

Wright, H. Norman. *Communication: Key to Your Marriage*. Ventura, California: Regal Books, 1974.

Chapter Eleven

Schaeffer, Edith. *What Is a Family?* Old Tappan, New Jersey: Fleming H. Revell Co., 1975.

Chapter Twelve

Howell, John. *Teaching Your Children about Sex*. Nashville, Tennessee: Broadman Press, 1973.

Chapter Fourteen

Dobson, James. *Dare to Discipline*. Wheaton, Illinois: Tyndale House Publishers, Inc., 1970.

Chapter Fifteen
Highlander, Don H. *Positive Parenting*. Waco, Texas: Word Books, 1980.

Chapter Sixteen
MacGregor, Malcolm. *Training Your Children to Handle Money*. Minneapolis, Minnesota: Bethany Fellowship, Inc., 1980.

Chapter Eighteen
Juroe, David and Juroe, Bonnie B. *Successful Step-Parenting*. Old Tappan, New Jersey: Fleming H. Revell Co., 1983.
Shedd, Charlie W. *Talk to Me*. Old Tappan, New Jersey: Spire Books, 1975.

Other Living Books Best-sellers

400 CREATIVE WAYS TO SAY I LOVE YOU by Alice Chapin. Perhaps the flame of love has almost died in your marriage, or you have a good marriage that just needs a little spark. Here is a book of creative, practical ideas for the woman who wants to show the man in her life that she cares. 07-0919-5

ANSWERS by Josh McDowell and Don Stewart. In a question-and-answer format, the authors tackle sixty-five of the most-asked questions about the Bible, God, Jesus Christ, miracles, other religions, and Creation. 07-0021-X

THE BELOVED STRANGER by Grace Livingston Hill. Graham came into her life at a desperate time, then vanished. But Sherrill could not forget the handsome stranger who captured her heart. 07-0303-0

BUILDING YOUR SELF-IMAGE by Josh McDowell and Don Stewart. Here are practical answers to help you overcome your fears, anxieties, and lack of self-confidence. Learn how God's higher image of who you are can take root in your heart and mind. 07-1395-8

THE CHILD WITHIN by Mari Hanes. The author shares insights she gained from God's Word during her own pregnancy, identifying areas of stress, offering concrete data about the birth process, and pointing to God's promises to lead those who are with young. 07-0219-0

CHRISTIANITY: THE FAITH THAT MAKES SENSE by Dennis McCallum. Ideal for new teachers and group study, this readable apologetic presents a clear, rational defense for Christianity to those unfamiliar with the Bible and challenges readers to meet Christ personally. 07-0525-4

COME BEFORE WINTER AND SHARE MY HOPE by Charles R. Swindoll. A collection of brief vignettes offering hope and the assurance that adversity and despair are temporary setbacks we can overcome! 07-0477-0

DAWN OF THE MORNING by Grace Livingston Hill. Dawn Rensselaer is a runaway bride, fleeing a man she was tricked into marrying. But is she also running away from love? 07-0530-0

Other Living Books Best-sellers

DR. DOBSON ANSWERS YOUR QUESTIONS by Dr. James Dobson. In this convenient reference book, renowned author Dr. James Dobson addresses heartfelt concerns on many topics, including questions on marital relationships, infant care, child discipline, home management, and others. 07-0580-7

DR. DOBSON ANSWERS YOUR QUESTIONS: RAISING CHILDREN by Dr. James Dobson. A renowned authority on child-rearing offers his expertise on the spiritual training of children, sex education, discipline, coping with adolescence, and more. 07-1104-1

THE EFFECTIVE FATHER by Gordon MacDonald. A practical study of effective fatherhood based on biblical principles. 07-0669-2

FOR MEN ONLY edited by J. Allan Petersen. This book deals with topics of concern to every man: the business world, marriage, fathering, spiritual goals, and problems of living as a Christian in a secular world. 07-0892-X

FOR WOMEN ONLY by Evelyn R. and J. Allan Petersen. This balanced, entertaining, and diversified treatment covers all the aspects of womanhood. 07-0897-0

GIVERS, TAKERS, AND OTHER KINDS OF LOVERS by Josh McDowell and Paul Lewis. Bypassing generalities about love and sex, this book answers the basics: Whatever happened to sexual freedom? Do men respond differently than women? Here are straight answers about God's plan for love and sexuality. 07-1031-2

HINDS' FEET ON HIGH PLACES by Hannah Hurnard. A classic allegory of a journey toward faith that has sold more than a million copies! 07-1429-6

HOW TO BE HAPPY THOUGH MARRIED by Tim LaHaye. A valuable resource that tells how to develop physical, mental, and spiritual harmony in marriage. 07-1499-7

JOHN, SON OF THUNDER by Ellen Gunderson Traylor. In this saga of adventure, romance, and discovery, travel with John—the disciple whom Jesus loved—down desert paths, through the courts of the Holy City, and to the foot of the cross as he leaves his luxury as a privileged son of Israel for the bitter hardship of his exile on Patmos. 07-1903-4

Other Living Books Best-sellers

LIFE IS TREMENDOUS! by Charlie "Tremendous" Jones. Believing that enthusiasm makes the difference, Jones shows how anyone can be happy, involved, relevant, productive, healthy, and secure in the midst of a high-pressure, commercialized society. 07-2184-5

MORE THAN A CARPENTER by Josh McDowell. A hard-hitting book for people who are skeptical about Jesus' deity, his resurrection, and his claim on their lives. 07-4552-3

QUICK TO LISTEN, SLOW TO SPEAK by Robert E. Fisher. Families are shown how to express love to one another by developing better listening skills, finding ways to disagree without arguing, and using constructive criticism. 07-5111-6

REASONS by Josh McDowell and Don Stewart. In a convenient question-and-answer format, the authors address many of the commonly asked questions about the Bible and evolution. 07-5287-2

RUTH, A LOVE STORY by Ellen Gunderson Traylor. Though the pain of separation and poverty would come upon her, Ruth was to become part of the very fulfillment of prophecy—and find true love as well. A biblical novel. 07-5809-9

THE SECRET OF LOVING by Josh McDowell. McDowell explores the values and qualities that will help both the single and married reader to be the right person for someone else. He offers a fresh perspective for evaluating and improving the reader's love life. 07-5845-5

THE STORY FROM THE BOOK. From Adam to Armageddon, this book captures the full sweep of the Bible's content in abridged, chronological form. Based on *The Book,* the best-selling, popular edition of *The Living Bible.* 07-6677-6

STRIKE THE ORIGINAL MATCH by Charles Swindoll. Swindoll draws on the best marriage survival guide–the Bible–and his 35 years of marriage to show couples how to survive, flex, grow, forgive, and keep romance alive in their marriage. 07-6445-5

THE STRONG-WILLED CHILD by Dr. James Dobson. With practical solutions and humorous anecdotes, Dobson shows how to discipline an assertive child without breaking his spirit. Parents will learn to overcome feelings of defeat or frustration by setting boundaries and taking action. 07-5924-9

Other Living Books Best-sellers

SUCCESS! THE GLENN BLAND METHOD by Glenn Bland. The author shows how to set goals and make plans that really work. His ingredients of success include spiritual, financial, educational, and recreational balances. 07-6689-X

TRANSFORMED TEMPERAMENTS by Tim LaHaye. An analysis of Abraham, Moses, Peter, and Paul, whose strengths and weaknesses were made effective when transformed by God. 07-7304-7

THROUGH GATES OF SPLENDOR by Elisabeth Elliot. This unforgettable story of five men who braved the Auca Indians has become one of the most famous missionary books of all time. 07-7151-6

WHAT WIVES WISH THEIR HUSBANDS KNEW ABOUT WOMEN by Dr. James Dobson. The best-selling author of *Dare to Discipline* and *The Strong-Willed Child* brings us this vital book that speaks to the unique emotional needs and aspirations of today's woman. An immensely practical, interesting guide. 07-7896-0

WHY YOU ACT THE WAY YOU DO by Tim LaHaye. Discover how your temperament affects your work, emotions, spiritual life, and relationships, and learn how to make improvements. 07-8212-7

You can find Tyndale books at fine bookstores everywhere. If you are unable to find these titles at your local bookstore, you may write for ordering information to:

Tyndale House Publishers
Tyndale Family Products Dept.
Box 448
Wheaton, IL 60189